Hope for the

Depressed

Overcoming Depression

Complete list of Christian books by Gary Schulz

Hope for the Depressed
Become a Biblical Marriage Counselor
May They Be One
Relationships —Why Jesus Came
From God's Perspective
From Victim to Victory
The Discipling Father
Setting the Captives Free
New Wine New Wineskins
God's Creation of the Sexual Union
If You Love Me...
Partners
Saved from our Enemies
Good News of Jesus Christ
Eternal Life What Is It?
God's Creation of Work
The Power Of God's Grace
God's Creation, The Family
Marriage Enrichment
Passing Your Faith
Freedom From Anger
Clearly Seen
Creation to Rebellion to Restoration
Oil In Your Lamp
Wimps!
Controlling Parent Controlling Child
Restoring Broken Walls

Hope for the

Depressed

Overcoming Depression

Gary Schulz

Kingdom Come Publications
81 Oaklawn Dr.
Midland, MI 48640

Printed in the United State of America

Contents

CONTENTS

Chapter 1

What Is Depression?

Every human being has experienced depression at some level. For most of us, depression is not life consuming. And for most, even if we had a serious bought of depression, it was short-lived and temporary. But for many, depression is a serious struggle that can rob us of contentment, happiness and a functional life. It has the ability to cripple us, and once we are consumed by it, it can destroy relationships, careers, health and any hope of a normal, happy and productive life. In any two week period, nearly 8 out of every 100 people of the age of 12 or older experiences moderate to severe depression.[1]

Depression is difficult to define because it is a painful feeling that comes from the inner man and permeates to our state of being. It begins in the heart, but affects the whole being. Depression is mostly a spiritual condition in that it resides in our thoughts and emotions. But what is depression? Where does it come from? What causes it? And more importantly, how do we overcome depression?

The medical community has identified the brain chemistry associated with depression. I don't want to dismiss their findings. For some of us, our chemistry may be off kilter and we may need to medicate. On the other hand, we cannot separate our spiritual and mental beings from our physical being. Brain chemistry may affect our mental and spiritual state. But the converse can also be true. Our brain chemistry can be affected by our mental and spiritual state. They work in cooperation with each other. And

---

[1] Pratt, L., & Brody, D. (2014). *Depression in the U.S. household population, 2009-2012* (Vol. 172). National Center for Health Statistics.

once it is out of balance, it can be a downhill slide. Medication may even be beneficial in severe cases so that we can focus on our spiritual and mental state, which may be the root cause of our struggles.

Whether we are on depression medication or not, the state of our mind and heart must be dealt with if we are to have any hope of long-term victory. Ultimate victory and ultimate cure is not measured by brain chemistry; it is identified by the state of our thinking and emotions. So this study does not start with a medical condition, but, rather, a spiritual and mental condition. Depression is a mental and spiritual condition.

So What Is Depression and What Causes It?

Depression is a painful spiritual state of being that is brought about because one or several spiritual needs are not being met, or at least they are perceived as not being met. So let's investigate how God has made us. Let's discuss the needs that we all have that can bring about depression if not met. All of us struggle to have our needs met. This is not a clearly defined area that can be quantified for each individual. Our beings are complex, and we were not all created the same. And the degree to which our needs are not met varies from person to person. And the combinations of unmet needs also vary. This is a complex understanding. But if we identify our God-given needs, maybe we can identify the sources of our depression and discover what we can do about it.

Man was created with several basic spiritual needs. Let's briefly go through some of them to get a picture of the potential causes of depression.

Need to love and be love

We all have a need to love others and to be loved by others. And with that said, we all fall short in our love for others, and consequently we all come short of the love we need. Simplistically, if love was perfected among us, depression would lose its crippling power. Sin is opposite of love, and we live in a world that is consumed by sin. Depression is death to the soul. In fact, depression is the leading cause of suicide. Love is the ultimate cure.

> We know that we have passed from death to life because we love our brothers. The one who does not love remains in death. 1 John 3:14 (HCSB)

If everyone suddenly became perfected in loving one another as Jesus loved us, we would not be able to imagine or be able to describe how uplifted we would all be in spirit. Unfortunately, in our present state, we do not live in a perfected world where love abounds and sin is no more. We wait for it in frustration.

> I consider that our present sufferings are not worth comparing with the glory that will be revealed in us. The creation waits in eager expectation for the sons of God to be revealed. **For the creation was subjected to frustration**, not by its own choice, but by the will of the one who subjected it, **in hope that the creation itself will be liberated from its bondage to decay and brought into the glorious freedom of the children of God.**
> **We know that the whole creation has been groaning as in the pains of childbirth right up to the present time**. Not only so, but we ourselves, who have the firstfruits of the Spirit, groan inwardly as we wait eagerly for our adoption as sons, the redemption of our bodies. For in this hope we were saved. But hope that is seen is no hope at all. Who hopes for what he already has? But if we hope for what we do not yet have, we wait for it patiently. Romans 8:18-25 (NIV)

Need to connect with people

We all have a need for other people in our lives. We all have a need to belong to a family and relatives. Depression can set in if we lose a loved one or experience a family breakup due to divorce or separation. We may grow old and experience children leaving home and moving far away and then, possibly, losing our spouse. Grieving is usually regarded as something different than depression, but many of the inner feelings can be very similar. When we lose a loved one, the grieving pain may be very intense, but typically we heal inside and the grieving passes with time. It is not a life-long struggle. But it is much like a special category of depression.

Depression has many emotions tied to it that mix together in varying proportions depending upon our situation. It could be despair, frustration, discouragement, rejection, loneliness, boredom, hopelessness, anger or hatred. This is what makes depression so difficult to understand and to discover the root causes and solutions. Our struggle in becoming connected with people is a major component.

We were created to be connected with people on an intimate level. Families were given to us to fill this God-given need. When this need is not fulfilled, we experience loneliness. Loneliness is a special form of depression that is extremely painful. Our God is compassionate and understands how he created us, for we were created in his image. He has a family too, the family of God, and we are his family. His heart goes out to the lonely, the widow and orphan. He becomes their father.

A father to the fatherless, a defender of widows, is God in his holy dwelling. God sets the lonely in families, he leads forth the prisoners with singing; but the rebellious live in a sun-scorched land. Psalm 68:5-6 (NIV)

The prisoners here can be prisoners of loneliness. Loneliness can be such an intense isolation that is like living in a prison cell with no escape.

Need for physical health

We all have physical bodies that we depend upon. Young people typically take their health for granted. They see themselves as if they will never grow old and lose their ability to function. Why do people smoke?

4

Don't they realize that they are planting the seeds of emphysema, heart disease and lung cancer? We just expect our bodies to continue to serve us. But eventually, we all lose our physical capacities. We all become old and lose our physical abilities to do the things we used to. And consequently, we become more isolated without the faculties to engage in life like we use to.

The occurrence of depression and suicide among the elderly is high.[2] The loss of health and loved ones can be very debilitating, with no hope of ever returning to the life we once joyfully possessed. By this time in their lives they have also lost much of their perceived purpose: career, raising children, skills, serving others and the like.

We don't expect to lose our physical capabilities when we are young, but it happens. We can have an accident or disease that handicaps us for the rest of our lives. Discouragement and hopelessness may set in. Our relationships with others are hampered now that we cannot do the things others engage in. Our hopes and dreams are altered. Our ability to work, provide and be productive can be suddenly cut off.

The state of our spirit and the state of our bodies are interdependent. Not only can bad health adversely affect our spirit; a depressed spirit can adversely affect the health of our bodies. And conversely, a cheerful heart can promote good health.

A cheerful heart is good medicine, but a broken spirit saps a person's strength. Proverbs 17:22 (NLT)

Need to live without pain

Normally, connected to our need for good health, we have a need to live without pain. Even a small splinter in our finger can take all of our attention. What about excruciating pain? I knew a man who had a head

---

[2] Center for Elderly Suicide Prevention - Crisis Hotline | Institute on Aging. (n.d.). Retrieved May 28, 2015, from http://www.ioaging.org/collaborations-elder-protection/center-for-elderly-suicide-prevention/

injury that caused him to get severe headaches. They came on every day and lasted several hours. He routinely had to leave work, go home to lie in bed while he suffered through headaches that were on the nine to ten level out of ten. This went on for decades before committing suicide.

Need for purpose

We all have a need for purpose. We do not just exist; we exist for purpose. We seek careers. We marry and have families. We serve God and mankind. We all fit into society in various forms, and we find purpose as we see the benefits that our lives bring to the welfare of the whole of society. When we lose purpose, we feel worthless and lose hope. We feel depressed.

What is boredom? Boredom can even be a segment of depression. God created us in his image. God is a creator. He is always about purpose.

> The LORD foils the plans of the nations; he thwarts the purposes of the peoples. But the plans of the LORD stand firm forever, the purposes of his heart through all generations. Psalm 33:10-11 (NIV)

> Many are the plans in a man's heart, but it is the LORD's purpose that prevails. Proverbs 19:21 (NIV)

Man was created for purpose. Boredom sets in when we sense that our time is being wasted on meaningless activity. Entertainment can fill this void for a time, but eventually we need the fulfillment of purpose. When we cannot see the purpose of our lives, depression can set in like darkness. Understanding our hearts in these times is very difficult, so our escape from depression becomes just as difficult.

> The purpose in a man's heart is like deep water, but a man of understanding will draw it out. Proverbs 20:5 (ESV)

Even if we discover that our depression is a result of our lack of purpose, we still have to discover our purpose. And then we have to pursue our purpose, which may be just as difficult. It may require finances, education and opportunities that are out of our control.

God promises to give us the desires of our hearts, but even this promise requires a relationship with and pursuit of God.

Delight yourself in the LORD, and he will give you the desires of your heart. Psalm 37:4 (ESV)

Need to succeed

We all have a need to succeed. Or, as another way of putting it; we all hate to fail. Let's think of some examples to get a clear picture.

Thousands of young people are going to college, and to do so they invest tens of thousands of dollars and four or more years of their lives with many long grueling hours of study. And after graduation they may find that they cannot get a job. And to make matters worse, they have thirty to fifty thousand dollars of student loans to pay back. Nearly half of college graduates find themselves in this situation. How do you think they feel? Failure and disappointment can bring about discouragement and breed all sorts of regret. Discouragement and despair can bring about depression.

Imagine the person who has labored for his employer, putting in long hours and doing all that he knows how to do, only to be one of those who has been let go from the company during a cost savings cutback. Now he must go home to tell his family. And in a tough labor market, he may not find another job, and he still has a mortgage to pay, bills and mouths to feed.

Consider the woman whose dream was to marry and have a house full of children. She eventually marries, but she cannot get pregnant. What a disappointment. Now that her dreams have been cut short, how does she handle the failure to become a mom?

What about the parents who loved their son and poured their lives into him, only to have him go astray in his teen years? Not only do they have to deal with their own failures, but they carry the burden of their son's failures.

Consider a lighter situation. Imagine working all day on your car because it suddenly did not start. And at the end of the day, it still does not start. You replaced parts and labored all day, only to have a car that still does not run, and now you do not have any other ideas for solving the problem. Think of the discouragement.

We all experience failures of various degrees. Seldom and minor failures are just part of this life, and most of us get past them. But what if the failures are not minor? What if they are frequent?

Need for physical security

We all have a need for physical security. We all struggle for survival and life is filled with responsibilities. Depression can set in if we lack the means for obtaining basic necessities, such as food, clothing, shelter, mobility and anything that we deem necessary for basic life existence. What happens if we lose our job? What if we cannot pay our bills and we lose our house or become evicted from our apartment? What if our car breaks down and we cannot afford the repairs?

We live in a competitive world where everyone is struggling to survive. We all want to increase our security, even at the expense of someone else's security. Gambling has been on a continual rise. People gamble with the hope of winning, but winning comes at the expense of all who lose. We are all subject to this drive for personal survival, and much of the time at the expense of others. We invest in the stock market, buying low and selling high. We are all seeking to be the winner, but someone has to be the loser. We strive for better and higher paying jobs. We form labor unions to demand higher wages at the expense of the corporation. We demand more and more from the government at the expense of those who pay the taxes.

In our struggle for security (or over indulgence of stuff) we borrow money for what we think we need for security and happiness. We borrow for a house, cars, furniture, appliances, and today we can buy most anything on time. Credit card debt has become a disease. We assume that we can buy now and pay later. But later comes and we cannot pay off our loans. We may have our possessions repossessed. Frustration and despair set in along with depression.

We live in a constant struggle for financial security. And when we lose the struggle, we can become hopelessly depressed.

Need for self-worth

We all struggle with who we are in the eyes of others and of ourselves. We struggle to be affirmed by others. And whether we are aware of it or not, we have a need to be affirmed by God, the one who made us. We were created as relational beings, and our value to others is part of our relationships. We have a need to belong to one another. We all live our lives in cooperation and dependence upon each other. We have different skills, strengths, likes and dislikes. Together, we form a living community. Our worth is seen in knowing how we fit into this living community and being appreciated for our personal contributions.

Much of that appreciation comes from those in authority over us. It begins at an early age when we look to the affirmation from our parents—especially fathers. Many—far too many—of us grew up in homes that lacked affirmation. In fact, they may have been places of rejection, abuse, disgust and many words that proclaimed our worthlessness: "You will never amount to anything!" "You're worthless!" "You're stupid!"

Sometimes parents project that we are unwanted through their behaviors, such as neglect, abandonment, divorce and a failure to take a positive interest in who we are, what we think, what we accomplish, what we enjoy or just our own unique personality.

It wasn't meant to be this way from the beginning, but because we all live with each other in a fallen, sinful world, we all struggle with a lack of affirmation, love and value by others. We all walk around wounded in this area of our soul, and we continually seek out affirmation like a starving person seeks out food. Depression is the pain of a starving soul.

Need for freedom

We have taken freedom for granted in the United States. Freedom is the ability to live day to day without confinement or the fear of reprisal or assault. It is the ability to go about life without being oppressed by someone in power or authority over us. It is the power to make personal choices based on our own will, as long as they do not negatively affect the welfare of others. It is the ability to live in peaceful harmony with others without fear.

The world we live in is in constant war and in fear of terrorists. The nightly news is consumed with updates on the conflicts that continue day after day. Millions of refugees flee from their homelands in fear of being ravaged. Evidence of ethnic cleansing in various countries fills recent history.

Our own country may not be experiencing war on our own turf, but crime leaves us in constant concern for protection of our lives and possessions. There are about 16,000 murders every year in the United States.[3] There are nearly 80,000 rapes.[4] There are about 345,000 robberies with an average individual loss of property at about $1,100.[5] The list goes on: aggravated assault, drug trafficking, drunk drivers on the road, extortion and any violation of our personal freedoms. Locking our doors is just a way of life.

---

[3] Assault or Homicide. (2015, February 6). Retrieved May 31, 2015, from http://www.cdc.gov/nchs/fastats/homicide.htm
[4] (2014, October 8). Retrieved May 31, 2015, from http://www.fbi.gov/about-us/cjis/ucr/crime-in-the-u.s/2013/crime-in-the-u.s.-2013/violent-crime/rape
[5] (2014, September 9). Retrieved May 31, 2015, from http://www.fbi.gov/about-us/cjis/ucr/crime-in-the-u.s/2013/crime-in-the-u.s.-2013/violent-crime/robbery-topic-page

Many of these offenders are caught and sentenced to prison. Prison is a place where nearly all freedom is removed. In fact, most of the needs listed here are not accessible for prisoners. And as a consequence, depression is a major struggle. In fact, most prisoners lacked many of these basic needs from childhood, and crime became a way of life. Now they find themselves in prison, where the provision for basic needs are even less. Depression can become overwhelming.

Need for hope in the future

Most of us can endure suffering, many hardships and setbacks if we just have hope that things will get better.

We were all created with a need for hope. Hope is the security we experience when we look down the road into our future, and can see a good outcome. For example, a young person may go to college to acquire skills for a desired career. He invests his money, energy and time into his studies with the hope of a well-paying and satisfying career. Once in his career, he may put money into a retirement account with the hope of one day leaving his career and being able to rest in his past labors to enjoy his final years of retirement. Hope is being confident in a good future for one's self. When hope is lost, depression sets in.

A person who gives of himself to love others, and who himself is loved by others, who has many meaningful connections with others, who has purpose for his own existence, who is physically secure and has hope in his future—show us such a person, and we will find that he is not likely to struggle with depression.

Depression can be complex because there are so many potential contributors. So, how do we define depression? What is it?

Depression is our inner pain of discouragement and hopelessness as a consequence of disappointing life situations in which we feel we cannot change or control. Depression is the pain we may feel when our needs are lacking. Depression and encouragement are opposites.

Reflection Questions

How often are you depressed or feel badly, discouraged or despondent?

What are your major sources of depression? Which of your needs are not being met?

How do you deal with your depression?

Chapter 2

Myopic Thinking

How big is a life? How do we even begin to quantify our lives? There are so many facets to life: job, career, financial status, health, skills, hobbies, recreation, friends, spouse, children, age, religion, culture, country, climate, home, possessions, abilities, opportunities, attractions, enjoyments and the list goes on. Our lives are extremely complex. Imagine dividing your life into two categories: positives and negatives. This becomes even more difficult because what is considered positive or negatives is a reflection of our attitudes and viewpoints.

Considering these many facets of life, what happens when we are depressed? Depression drives us to focus on one or more negative aspects of our lives. We focus so much, that these few negative aspects become all consuming. We tend to see our lives as all hopelessly negative. We do not see the good or positive aspects because the negative overshadows them all. It is kind of like looking through a straw at a dark object. One eye is closed, so all it can see is dark. And the other eye is only focused on a dark spot. There may be all kinds of bright areas in all of the other directions, but for now all we see is dark. Our lives are not completely dark, but if the focus of our heart and mind is only on the dark portion, that is all that we will see.

These dark spots consume our thinking; all mental attention is given to them. And if we allow ourselves to linger there, we will eventually lose all hope that there is any bright spot in our lives. For example, the man who just got fired from his job while he has a wife and four children at home can be consumed with failure, fear and the disappointment of not having a new job. It may overwhelm his consciousness. His myopic thinking blinds him of the blessings of his wonderful wife, his beautiful children and his loyal friends. He discounts the skills and abilities that he has acquired over the years. His fear robs him of any optimism. There may be great possibilities for him, but he lacks the ability to see down the road into the future because he is focusing on the past failures and present consequences. He may even be angry inside. And all of this darkness consumes him and eats away at his soul. He is depressed!

Focus on God

If he would pick his head up he would see that all of life is not dark and hopeless. He would see that he has much to be thankful for. The Bible instructs us in many places to "lift up our eyes" and to see the Lord and what he has done and what he will yet do. He is our hope for a glorious future. In fact, he is our only hope. All else is just temporary and shortsighted.

Notice in the following verses that it says that we lift up our eyes. In other words, I am responsible to stop focusing on the dark spot of my life, but to put my focus up much higher than my little life and project my attention on God, who is life, and look up to him for my eternal destiny. All that exists has been made by God. He is the only one who is in complete control of all things. And he loves his children. We are to look to the maker of heaven and earth as a child looks to his loving father. Our lives are much bigger than these dark areas that we focus on. We need to consciously lift up our eyes to the Lord and maker of all that exists.

I lift up my eyes to the hills—where does my help come from? My help comes from the LORD, the Maker of heaven and earth. He will not let your foot slip—he who watches over you will not slumber; indeed, he who watches over Israel will neither slumber nor sleep. The LORD watches over you—the LORD is your shade at your right hand; the sun will not harm you by day, nor the moon by night. The LORD will keep you from all harm—he will watch over your life; the LORD will watch over your coming and going both now and forevermore. Psalm 121:1-8 (NIV)

How would you like personal access to the president of the United States? How would you like to be able to call him up whenever you were in need so that he could open a way for you whenever you needed an open door? Well, we have someone much greater than the president to call upon in our need. We can call upon God Almighty whose throne is above every throne. But we must lift our eyes to him.

I lift up my eyes to you, to you whose throne is in heaven. As the eyes of slaves look to the hand of their master, as the eyes of a maid look to the hand of her mistress, so our eyes look to the LORD our God, till he shows us his mercy. Psalm 123:1-2 (NIV)

Depression is a horrible state of captivity. We need to be rescued from depression. Lifting our eyes is a deliberate act of taking our eyes off of our weakness and focusing them on the loving power of the Most High God.

"Because he loves me," says the LORD, "I will rescue him; I will protect him, for he acknowledges my name. **He will call upon me, and I will answer him; I will be with him in trouble, I will deliver him and honor him**. With long life will I satisfy him and show him my salvation." Psalm 91:14-16 (NIV)

God refers to us as his children. Children don't worry about having food and clothing. They don't worry about having a house to live in. They don't worry about paying bills. They leave those concerns to their parents who provide and watch over them. We don't fret and worry until we have grown up and have taken on the many responsibilities of life. But from God's view, we are still children, and he is our all-powerful and loving Father. Much of the time our depression comes from our expectation to be responsible for things that are out of our control. Where do we find rest from these anxieties? The answer is to let God handle what is impossible for us. It is a matter of living out a child-to-Father relationship.

LORD, my heart is not proud; my eyes are not haughty. I do not get involved with things too great or too difficult for me. Instead, I have calmed and quieted myself like a little weaned child with its mother; I am like a little child. Psalm 131:1-2 (HCSB)

The Black Hole of Worry. What Is Worry?

Worry is a myopic view of our lives. When we worry we focus on one aspect of our lives, and we seem to be bound by our focus. We try to solve (escape) a problem by thinking about it over and over—usually making no progress. We think that somehow we possess within ourselves the means to figure our way out of our situation, but deliverance rarely comes. We are already frustrated, and eventually we may become hopeless. And hopelessness leads to depression.

Ironically, the problem we are trying to solve in our minds is not our greatest problem. The biggest struggle is maintaining peace and perspective of our lives. When we worry, we become so myopically focused that we disengage from the rest of our lives. We cannot see the value in other aspects.

Most of us have seen the classic movie, *It's A Wonderful Life*. George Bailey is a bank owner. He didn't want to run a bank, but he inherited it from his father, and now he was stuck with it and stuck in the same old town. To make matters worse, a great deal of money was lost, and now all of the depositors wanted their money, and so the bank was about to collapse. Worry set in on George Bailey, but that was not his greatest loss. His devaluation of his own life and all of God's blessings robbed him of what truly counted in his life. After worrying and trying everything in his own power to escape, he gave up in failure. He walked around in depression, frustration and anger—destroying all of his once valuable relationships with his wife, children and friends. He complained about his house and cursed his own life. To George Bailey, his life was worthless and not worth living. So he attempted suicide.

But God rescued him through Clarence, an angel. Clarence takes George through a journey of what life in his town and his family would have been like if he had never lived. He then sees all of the people that were blessed because of his life. He is given a chance to see what life would have been like if he had not been there. It was then that George saw how he had blessed others throughout his life, through his life. Then he began to see that people were much more important than the failure of his bank.

Clarence the angel said, "You see, George, you've really had a wonderful life. Don't you see what a mistake it would be to throw it away?"

"Strange, isn't it? Each man's life touches so many other lives. When he isn't around he leaves an awful hole, doesn't he?"

Worry is the mental activity of focusing on the terrible problems of life and missing all of the wonderful blessings. We miss the value of others and our value to others. In our struggle to solve life's struggles, we miss true life. Depression robs us of our appreciation of life.

Jesus understood life. He appreciated and highly valued life from the view of relationships. He understood that our first focus needed to be God's kingdom and God's righteousness here on earth. And he implores us to take the same view of our lives.

This is why I tell you: Don't worry about your life, what you will eat or what you will drink; or about your body, what you will wear. Isn't life more than food and the body more than clothing? Look at the birds of the sky: They don't sow or reap or gather into barns, yet your heavenly Father feeds them. Aren't you worth more than they? Can any of you add a single cubit to his height by worrying? And why do you worry about clothes? Learn how the wildflowers of the field grow: they don't labor or spin thread. Yet I tell you that not even Solomon in all his splendor was adorned like one of these! If that's how God clothes the grass of the field, which is here today and thrown into the furnace tomorrow, won't He do much more for you—you of little faith? So don't worry, saying, 'What will we eat?' or 'What will we drink?' or 'What will we wear?' For the idolaters eagerly seek all these things, and your heavenly Father knows that you need them. But seek first the kingdom of God and His righteousness, and all these things will be provided for you. Therefore don't worry about tomorrow, because tomorrow will worry about itself. Each day has enough trouble of its own. Matthew 6:25-34 (HCSB)

Worry is the mental battle of trying to fix a problem that is out of our control to fix. We mull it over in our minds until it wears us down. We worry about tomorrow, and miss today. And when tomorrow comes, we miss that day as well as we worry about the next tomorrow. It is a fruitless, endless struggle that does not resolve anything. And all this time we have a loving God who waits for us to call out to him. The fact is that we are all weak, and God is without any weakness. Furthermore, he loves us beyond our understanding.

The Black Hole of Failure

Our lives are complex. Our lives have many parts, and each part may be functioning just fine—except one. So we have a tendency to focus on that one failing part. We focus so intently that, in time, the dark spot seems to engulf our entire life. We lose the ability to see anything good in our life.

Many men (and women) experience what has been called a mid-life crisis when they are in their forties. In their twenties and thirties they may have had dreams and expectations about their wonderful future. He may have dreamed about his advancing career. She may have been dreaming about establishing a beautiful, loving family. They may have dreamed of having a beautiful home with a life that just keeps getting better.

But by the time they are in their forties, the dreams should be coming true. If not, time is running out, and these dreams for a glorious future are not likely anymore. Maybe you did not progress in your career as you thought. Or maybe you did progress, but the satisfaction was not there, and you realized that you were just "chasing the carrot on the end of the stick" with little fulfillment. Maybe you had dreams of having a houseful of children, but you couldn't get pregnant. Or maybe you had those children, but they got caught up in all of the sins of the world, and their lives are a wreck. Or maybe you had two children in your early twenties, and now in your early forties your children are gone and you are back to a void in your life, and now you have no dreams for your future to fill the emptiness. Maybe you dreamed of that nice house, cars, boat and most things that money can buy. Now you have them, but your life is still empty. Now what?

When you were young, you were inspired by the hope of what the future would bring. But now the future is today, and today is not as fulfilling as the dreams you once had. Hopeless failure is all that you see for your life. It consumes your thinking and emotions. Your failure to achieve your dreams becomes your life. Failure becomes your black hole, and you do not see any light around you because you are so focused on the dark hole that you cannot see anything else in your life. Even if there are good things, you cannot see them. Your life appears to you as nothing but darkness.

Many try to escape their black hole by foolishly doing something desperate. They may quit their job and desperately try to be fulfilled with another dream. They may begin to think that they are married to the wrong person, so they seek out an affair. And the affair may result in divorcing the spouse of their youth to pursue another spouse of their dreams. In time, they realize that they were just chasing a dream, and missed reality. Some will try to escape by pursuing adventure. Maybe they will buy a motor cycle and all of the biker clothing. Then they may join a club with others who are pursuing the same. Together they are hoping to find happiness. But as time passes, contentment and satisfaction do not come.

Failure to achieve our dreams and expectations can become a myopic black hole, to which there seems to be no escape.

The Black Hole of Loneliness

We were all created with a need for people in our lives. God is a relational being, and we were created in his image. Having meaningful relationships is one of our most fundamental and essential needs. When our lives are void of these relationships, we become lonely. This subject will be covered more deeply in another chapter, but let's focus on the myopic aspect.

Myopic loneliness occurs among all age groups. Teenagers are in constant competition for group acceptance and inclusion. An intact, loving family is his greatest security, but with divorce, out-of-wedlock births and working parents, too many teens are left to themselves. Suicide among teens is one of the leading causes of their death.

Divorce has left many alone without a family. Being single is not freedom. Being single leaves one in a constant pursuit of connecting with others. Family is what they yearn, but they are without.

People are forgoing marriage in order to pursue a career. The career may happen, but the family does not. And the career cannot fill the empty voids of loneliness. The sexual union was created by God for marriage, but most adults experience extramarital sex. But intercourse does not provide a family with deep, lasting committed relationships. An intimate relationship with one partner fills our need. The pursuit of multiple partners with no lasting commitment does not fill it, but only leaves one in a constant pursuit.

As we get old, we may lose our spouse to death, if we have not already lost him or her to divorce. And the older we get, we begin to lose our older friends to death. We can find ourselves all alone. And what hope is there at this point to establish a new family?

We all struggle for acceptance, but we all have felt the pain of rejection. God may have created us for relationships, but we live in a sinful state in a sinful world. Sin is relational. Sin is anything that is contrary to intimate relationships. In this regard, we all struggle with ourselves and with others. We are all in this life struggle which does not end. We can't ignore it, and it can consume us. It can become our entire focus, and while we are in this hole, we don't see much light. If we look out of the hole, all that we think we see is that others all have what we long for. But this is a deception. Everyone struggles with their need for others.

The Black Hole of Loss

We live on hope. Man is the only creature of God's creation that looks out into the future. He is the only one who plans for tomorrow—next week—next year—and even decades out into our future lives. God created us this way. We live on hope, and we are all striving to have a hope that will sustain us.

But what if our hopes were just unfulfilled fantasies? Now what? Hope is filled with optimism. It lights up our lives. But unfulfilled hopes are darkness. They leave us without hope. Our lives become dark, and that is all that we can see for our future.

For example, we have one divorce for every two marriages in the United States. This is true for Christian or non-Christian. I would suspect that nearly all of those who marry and exchange vows had a glorious hope of uniting together in marriage with joyful expectations for their future; this was their hope. But now they have been married several years, and the rosy future is not so rosy anymore. Tension mounts. Offenses are harbored. The hope they once had is dwindling. Then the one with the least hope leaves and files for divorce. How does that make you feel? Life becomes dark and lonely. The loss of your marriage is devastating. If you were a child of your parents' divorce, the loss may be even more devastating.

Loss of the marriage bond is like losing a part of your life. It does not have to come by divorce. You may lose your spouse by death. Now there is clearly no hope of getting him or her back. You have to go on with a significant part of you missing. Loss can be crushing, and it can rob us of hope. We feel two pains at the same time: the loss of a marriage partner, and the hopeless view of the future.

Any significant loss can take a toll on our hearts. Marriage is one example, but what about the loss of a job or career? What if you were let go from your job after twenty-five years in the company. Other companies are looking for younger men, and it is too late to acquire new skills to make you competitively employable. You are too young to retire and you still have financial responsibilities. The loss has left you hopeless with no obvious options available. The future looks bleak, and your life looks dark. You cannot see anything but darkness in your life.

There are many other devastating losses that can create for us a black hole of myopic focus. Many lose their health. It could be a stroke or heart attack, cancer, diabetes, arthritis, paralysis or any one of a number of health problems. Why has health insurance become such a big part of our lives? We are trying to protect ourselves from unwanted, devastating loss.

What if life seemed to be going along normally, and then you found yourself caught up in a crime and you were sentenced to years in prison? It happens all the time. You could be falsely accused of sexual abuse. You could be involved in a car accident where someone was killed, and you had been drinking. I know hundreds of prisoners, and many never conceived that they would someday be caught up in a crime and sent to prison and become a felon.

We live in a litigatious society. What if you were sued and lost your financial foundation—your house and your savings. What if you retired early, and then the fall in the stock market cut your retirement by 40%, and now you must go back to work—if you can find a job. You become a setup for dark myopic thinking that can consume you.

Many have had a life of abuse, shortcomings and disappointments. Their view of life and of themselves may not be optimistically hopeful. Every little setback becomes a setup for myopic thinking. They are crippled inside and see life as one black hole after another. Light may be shining all around them, but they cannot see it. To them, all is darkness, for that is their focus. That is the deception they live in.

God is light and hope. He promises to come near to all who call out to him truthfully from their hearts.

The LORD is near all who cry out to him, all who cry out to him sincerely. He satisfies the desire of his loyal followers; he hears their cry for help and delivers them. Psalm 145:18-19 (NET)

It is difficult to go through this life without sustaining some sort of loss. How do we maintain a bright hope in the midst of loss? Or maybe the question should be, "How do we see the light in our lives when a dark spot happens. How do we see light in the darkness?" As the psalmist wrote, God is near to those who cry out to him. He satisfies the desires of his "loyal followers", those who fear him, for he is the God who created all things. He is the final judge, and he is also the essence of love. He hears our cries for help, and only he has the power to deliver us from our darkness.

Grumbling and Complaining, the Seeds of Darkness

In order to answer the question of how to conquer dark myopic depression, let's take a look at the Israelites and how they discarded their hope while in the midst of hardships in the crossing of the desert going from their bondage in Egypt to the Promised Land.

The Israelites had a marvelous future ahead of them, as promised by God. They were promised a land of their own that was lush with hills and water and beauty and vegetation beyond imagination. God delivered them from four hundred years of slavery in Egypt. He showed his almighty arm with ten plaques and the parting of the Red Sea. Then he led them on a journey across the desert to get to the land he promised. Even in the desert he provided food, water, protection, guidance and leaders. There was hardship. But in the midst of the hardship, God provided for every need. And the journey was taking them to a lush land where they would find peace, joy and rest.

But they did not focus on the promise or the hand of God upon them. All that the Israelites saw was the desert. They grumbled and complained the entire way. When they finally got to the Promised Land, they discovered that it was already inhabited. God told them to go in and take it for themselves, and that he would go before them and give them victory. But they did not believe him, and they grumbled and complained again, accusing Moses and God of leading them across the desert, only to be killed by these foreign people.

Their focus was always on what they deemed as a failure to get what they desired. They did not trust and believe God, so they did not see how he was protecting and providing for them. They did not see that God was in the process of blessing them. It would have been easy if they were instantly transplanted from slavery to the lush land of promise. But that is not how God was going to do it. In order to receive the blessings, they needed to endure the struggle with thankfulness and trust that God loved them and would deliver them by his strength. The Israelites failed the test. Instead of entering the Promised Land in just a few weeks of travel across the desert, God sent them back to the desert for forty years. They all died in the desert and their children received the land of promise.

We are warned not to fail in our lives as the children of God failed to enter God's rest. They failed because their hearts became hard toward God. And when their hearts became hard, they grumbled, complained, disobeyed, rebelled and lost faith in God. [Read the following verses to get a clear picture of their grumbling and complaining: Exodus 15:24-17:3, Numbers 14:1-36, 16:11, 16:41 17:5, 17:10, Deut. 1:27, Psalm 78, Psalm 106:25] We need to heed the warning not to fail as the Israelites did.

> Therefore, as the Holy Spirit says: Today, if you hear His voice, do not harden your hearts as in the rebellion, on the day of testing in the wilderness, where your fathers tested Me, tried [Me], and saw My works for 40 years. Therefore I was provoked with that generation and said, "They always go astray in their hearts, and they have not known My ways." So I swore in My anger, "They will not enter My rest."
> Watch out, brothers, so that there won't be in any of you an evil, unbelieving heart that departs from the living God. But encourage each

other daily, while it is still called today, so that none of you is hardened by sin's deception. For we have become companions of the Messiah if we hold firmly until the end the reality that we had at the start. As it is said:

> Today, if you hear His voice, do not harden your hearts as in the rebellion.

For who heard and rebelled? Wasn't it really all who came out of Egypt under Moses? And who was He provoked with for 40 years? Was it not with those who sinned, whose bodies fell in the wilderness? And who did He swear to that they would not enter His rest, if not those who disobeyed? So we see that they were unable to enter because of unbelief. Hebrews 3:7-19 (HCSB)

Therefore, while the promise to enter His rest remains, let us fear that none of you should miss it. For we also have received the good news just as they did; but the message they heard did not benefit them, since they were not united with those who heard it in faith (for we who have believed enter the rest), in keeping with what He has said:

> So I swore in My anger, they will not enter My rest.

And yet His works have been finished since the foundation of the world, for somewhere He has spoken about the seventh day in this way:

> And on the seventh day God rested from all His works.

Again, in that passage [He says], They will never enter My rest. Since it remains for some to enter it, and those who formerly received the good news did not enter because of disobedience, again, He specifies a certain day—today—speaking through David after such a long time, as previously stated:

> Today, if you hear His voice, do not harden your hearts.

For if Joshua had given them rest, God would not have spoken later about another day. Therefore, a Sabbath rest remains for God's people. For the person who has entered His rest has rested from his own works, just as God did from His. Let us then make every effort to enter that rest, so that no one will fall into the same pattern of disobedience. Hebrews 4:1-11 (HCSB)

What is our bondage of slavery? How is God delivering us? What is our desert experience? What is our Promised Land, and what enemies do we need to conquer in God's strength? How are we focusing in what God has already done for us? How thankful have we been throughout our struggles? Have we focused on our blessings, or have we complained? *Has the dark spot of our life become our only focus such that we do not see anything good—anything that comes from God. Do we not see the hand of God in our lives in the midst of suffering?* Complaining is something we do. It may not be consciously premeditated, but complaining is still a choice. And it is a choice to focus on what is bad (from our perspective). It is myopic thinking. We make a choice to focus on what is dark in our lives. We can choose to focus on what is dark to the extent that we lose focus on anything that provides light for our lives. Or we can choose to focus on what is good, on what God provides for us out of his love for us. Complaining by itself can destroy our own lives from within. It becomes a myopic captivity.

How do we stop? There are two actions. The first is to stop complaining. Stop focusing on every dark spot. Stop creating dark spots in your mind.

Do everything without complaining or arguing, so that you may become blameless and pure, children of God without fault in a crooked and depraved generation, in which you shine like stars in the universe as you hold out the word of life—in order that I may boast on the day of Christ that I did not run or labor for nothing. Philippians 2:14-16 (NIV)

The second step is to start being thankful. Deliberately focus on all that is good.

Thankfulness—Focusing on the Light

Myopic thinking is a focus on all that is dark in your life. This intense focus is a lie, and it robs us of all hope for the future. How do we escape the lie, especially when we consider that the lie manifests in our own thinking.

This lie has two dimensions. The first is exaggeration. For example, if a person is fired from his job, he may conclude in his dark and hopeless thinking that he will never find a new job, that he is a worthless failure, that he will probably lose his house and possessions, he may become a homeless beggar, that his family will no longer look up to him—and any other negative thing associated with losing a job.

That is one dimension of the lie. The other lie says that there is nothing good about my life. Our whole life becomes the dark spot such that we cannot see the good and positive aspects of our lives. We have all heard the saying of a glass being half empty or half full. An optimistic person sees the glass has half full. The pessimistic thinker sees it as half empty. The myopic thinker sees the glass as empty.

Apostle Paul was falsely accused and put into prison for several years. But there is no indication that he suffered from depression. In fact, by his own words he was very optimistic and joyful. His chains robbed him of his freedom, but he saw past his confinement and saw the good that was resulting from his imprisonment.

> I want you to know, brothers and sisters, that my situation has actually turned out to advance the gospel: The whole imperial guard and everyone else knows that I am in prison for the sake of Christ, and most of the brothers and sisters, having confidence in the Lord because of my imprisonment, now more than ever dare to speak the word fearlessly. Philippians 1:12-14 (NET)

This comes from his letter to the Christian Philippians. And in this same letter he implores them to rejoice and to be thankful, and he tells them what to think about in these perilous times of intense persecution.

Rejoice in the Lord always. Again I say, rejoice! Let everyone see your gentleness. The Lord is near! **Do not be anxious about anything. Instead**, in every situation, through prayer and petition **with thanksgiving,** tell your requests to God. **And the peace of God that surpasses all understanding will guard your hearts and minds in Christ Jesus**.

Finally, brothers and sisters, whatever is true, whatever is worthy of respect, whatever is just, whatever is pure, whatever is lovely, whatever is commendable, if something is excellent or praiseworthy, think about these things. Philippians 4:4-8 (NET)

This one passage—if applied—is sufficient to deliver anyone from depressive myopic thinking. So let's take a closer look at his focus.

First, in any situation, "the Lord is near", so rejoice. The almighty God loves us and is at our side. He is well aware of our situations, pain and struggles. He has not abandoned us. Just because we are experiencing a painful trial does not mean that God has removed his hand from our lives or that he does not love us. Think about Paul; he is writing from prison. Paul emphasizes that we should exuberantly rejoice in the Lord. This means to verbally proclaim that he is near, and to lift his name up. We are to proclaim his attributes: his power, his wisdom, his patience, his love for us, his protection, and his provision. We are to remember all that he has done in our lives and all that he has done over the millennium to fulfill his purposes. And we are an integral part of all that he is accomplishing, for we are his children. We belong to him as his beloved.

This rejoicing is the deliberate act of lifting our heads to God and focusing on the much bigger picture. When we do this, we find that our present suffering—as painful as it might be—is only a tiny spec of our entire eternal lives in Christ Jesus.

So Paul implores us to realize and focus on the fact that God is near and involved in our circumstances. He is not distant, uninvolved or disinterested. And because of this fact, he instructs us not to be "anxious about anything".

He uses a very strong and important word: "Instead". Instead of being anxious, "in every situation" we call out to God in prayer. But Paul instructs us not to just present our requests, but to call out with thanksgiving. What does that mean? We are in pain; so what are we to be thankful for? The point is that we always have much to be thankful for. Myopic thinking tells us that all is bad, and that there is nothing good to be thankful for. Part of our praise and worship of God is to proclaim his goodness and love for us.

Remember how he delivered his chosen people from 400 years of slavery in Egypt, performed many miracles along the way, provided food and water in the desert and brought them safely to the Promised Land. And what did they do? They complained incessantly about how God did not love them because they were in a desert. What is your desert? Thankfulness is our conscious proclamation of how God loves us. It is much more than just saying that he loves us. It is citing specific real examples from our lives, examples that coexist with our state of suffering.

I have personally heard many prisoners express how thankful they are that they woke up today, that they had a bed to sleep in, that they had food to eat, and most importantly that he saved their lives, both physical and spiritually for eternity. Most of these prisoners will profess that if left on the street, they would be dead by now. If left on the street, their souls would still be lost. Our lives are not all dark. How has God blessed you? Proclaim how God has been good to you. That is what it means to be thankful. *Myopic thinking is being totally unthankful by proclaiming that all of your life is dark and miserable.* Like the Israelites in the desert, we can even be spiteful toward God, denying his love for us by not recognizing anything good in our lives.

Paul makes a very significant promise for those who call out to God with a thankful attitude. He wrote that they would receive the peace of God that is beyond our understanding. In addition, this peace from God would act as a guard for our hearts and minds so that they remain focused on Christ Jesus. That sounds like a recipe to be delivered from depression!

Paul does not stop there. He continues by instructing us to be in control of our thoughts. It is easy to think negative and speak negative. Paul instructs us to think about things that are edifying to our souls. He gives us a list of what to focus on:

Whatever is true,

Whatever is worthy of respect,

whatever is just,

Whatever is pure,

Whatever is lovely,

Whatever is commendable,

If something is excellent or praiseworthy,

Think about these things.

Notice that this list is all positive things. Here is a list of things to focus on that is almost guaranteed to make you depressed:

Whatever is a lie about your life

Whatever rejects others

Whatever is morally filthy

Whatever is disgusting

Whatever is degrading of others

If there is anything to complain about or dishonor,

Think about such things.

Depression begins with our thinking. Our thoughts are not random and out of our ability to control. Paul wrote that we are to be transformed by the renewing of our minds. (Romans 12:2) This transformation is twofold. First, we need to have a new perspective of what is true. That is why we read God's word. That is why we seek wisdom and understanding from God and others. That is the intellectual side of a renewed mind. The other side is indentified by the self-control of our thoughts. We can choose to have negative thoughts, and we can choose to have positive ones. Paul instructs us to have positive ones.

If depression springs forth from our thoughts, and if we have dominion over our thoughts, then we can have dominion over depression.

Think about it; God has given us his own Spirit to live within us. And his Spirit knows what is happening to us. And the Spirit is praying for us. We have a glorious purpose—God's purpose. We are partakers of his kingdom to come, and he is working things out in conformity to a much bigger purpose that is beyond our present day circumstance. We can rejoice because we are included in his plans and purposes. We are loved by God—now in our suffering, and on into eternity where all suffering will be removed for those who are in Christ Jesus.

Likewise **the Spirit helps us in our weakness**. For we do not know what to pray for as we ought, but **the Spirit himself intercedes for us with groanings too deep for words**. And he who searches hearts knows what is the mind of the Spirit, because **the Spirit intercedes for the saints according to the will of God**. And we know that for **those who love God all things work together for good, for those who are called according to his purpose**. For those whom he foreknew he also predestined to be conformed to the image of his Son, in order that he might be the firstborn among many brothers. And those whom he predestined he also called, and those whom he called he also justified, and those whom he justified he also glorified.

What then shall we say to these things? **If God is for us, who can be against us?** He who did not spare his own Son but gave him up for us all, how will he not also with him graciously give us all things? Who shall bring any charge against God's elect? It is God who justifies. Who is to condemn? Christ Jesus is the one who died—more than that, who was raised—who is at the right hand of God, **who indeed is interceding for us. Who shall separate us from the love of Christ?** Shall tribulation, or distress, or persecution, or famine, or nakedness, or danger, or sword? As it is written, "For your sake we are being killed all the day long; we are regarded as sheep to be slaughtered." No, **in all these things we are more than conquerors through him who loved us**. For I am sure that neither death nor life, nor angels nor rulers, nor things present nor things to come, nor powers, nor height nor depth, nor anything else in all creation, **will be able to separate us from the love of God in Christ Jesus our Lord**. Romans 8:26-39 (ESV)

Reflection Questions

Describe your life in terms of what you think about most.

What do you worry about? Has your worry ever fixed anything? Describe how you take your concerns to your heavenly Father.

Do you feel like a failure? Describe how you have failed. How has your focus on failure crippled your chances of succeeding?

Are you lonely? How has loneliness consumed your life? Who are the closest people in your life? How have you sought them out during your struggles?

Have you had a significant loss in your life? How has it captivated your thinking?

Are you a complainer? Does your depression revolve around your thinking of your terrible life? Are you consumed with blaming others and circumstances for the shortcomings in your life?

What do you have to be thankful for? Make a list—make it as long as possible. Thank God—out loud—for everything good in your life.

Chapter 3

Self-Focus Can Be a Dark Hole

Show me an undisciplined child, and I will show you a spoiled child. Show me a spoiled child, and I will show you an unhappy child. Show me an adult who was spoiled as a child, and I will show you an unhappy adult. Show me an unhappy adult, and I will show you someone who is in a dark hole of self-focus. Show me a spoiled, self-focused adult, and I will show you someone who is prone to depression.

Self-Focus, the Root of Our Fall

Does this sound like a trap? It is! Selfishness is one of the greatest traps on earth. It began in the Garden of Eden. Eve couldn't have had more life. She had a perfect existence with all of the pleasant provisions of God. She had a husband, and God walked with them daily in this garden of paradise. There were no hardships. The garden was lush with food that could be picked right from the trees. There was no sickness, not even death. Their relationship with one another and with God was one of perfect love, peace and unity. It could not have been any better. But Eve was tempted by the possibility that there might be more. She knew God had more than her. After all, he was their provider, protector and he instructed them with his infinite wisdom. She also knew that she was dependent upon God for life, and therefore she was under his authority—he ruled; she didn't. Eve was tempted with the thought of what it would be like if she was the focus with all of God's powers and wisdom. Maybe she could experience life without God if she only had what he had. Look at the account.

But the serpent said to the woman, "You will not surely die. For God knows that when you eat of it **your eyes will be opened, and you will be like God, knowing good and evil**." So when the woman saw that the tree was good for food, and that it was a delight to the eyes, and that the tree was to be desired to make one wise, she took of its fruit and ate, and she also gave some to her husband who was with her, and he ate. Genesis 3:4-6 (ESV)

Eve made a choice with her husband Adam to become independent of God. They wanted to be like him. The serpent (the devil) who tempted Eve had fallen to a similar temptation prior to this. The devil was once a magnificent angel who was anointed by God with the title of guardian cherub. Like Adam and Eve, he had a glorious existence as one of God's most high angels who served God. He walked with God on the holy mountain of God. He was created magnificent and blameless. (Ezekiel 28:14-15) But he began to self-focus on his magnificence and beauty, and he became proud. In ignorance, he succumbed to pride and lost his beauty, his magnificence and his high position with God.

Your heart became proud because of your beauty; For the sake of your splendor you corrupted your wisdom. So I threw you down to the earth; I made you a spectacle before kings. Ezekiel 28:17 (HCSB)

Self-focus is a root cause of our downfall. Self-focus is a root cause of sin. And self-focus is a root cause of depression. So how does this work?

Love Opposes a Self-Focus

To answer this question as to how a self-focus is a deep root of depression, let's first look at love. God is love. (1 John 4:6 & 16) How does love compare to being self-focused. Love is the act of living for the welfare of others. It is the act of giving up of my life so that someone else can have more life. We have discussed the devil and Eve's failure to live under God and for God. They failed because of the temptation to live for themselves and to raise themselves up. Now consider Jesus. Jesus was already higher than the devil or man. He was the Son of God. All things were created by him and for him. (Colossians 1:15-20) In comparison, instead of seeking independence of his heavenly Father and raising himself up, he did just the opposite. We are instructed to have his attitude.

Do nothing out of selfish ambition or vain conceit, but in humility consider others better than yourselves. Each of you should look not only to your own interests, but also to the interests of others.

Your attitude should be the same as that of Christ Jesus: Who, being in very nature God, did not consider equality with God something to be grasped, but made himself nothing, taking the very nature of a servant, being made in human likeness. And being found in appearance as a man, he humbled himself and became obedient to death—even death on a cross! Therefore God exalted him to the highest place and gave him the name that is above every name, that at the name of Jesus every knee should bow, in heaven and on earth and under the earth, and every tongue confess that Jesus Christ is Lord, to the glory of God the Father. Philippians 2:3-11 (NIV)

Notice that Jesus did not attempt to exalt himself as the devil and Eve had done. Rather, he lowered himself and became a servant in the hands of God to fulfill God's purposes and will. Later, however, God exalted Jesus. He exalted him because he obediently lowered himself and became an obedient servant—even unto rejection by man and death on a cross at the hands of men, whom he came to serve.

We are called to have the same attitude toward others as Jesus Christ. We are called to love others as Jesus loved.

This is how we know what love is: Jesus Christ laid down his life for us. And we ought to lay down our lives for our brothers. If anyone has material possessions and sees his brother in need but has no pity on him, how can the love of God be in him? Dear children, let us not love with words or tongue but with actions and in truth. 1 John 3:16-18 (NIV)

As Christ followers (Christians), we are called to love one another. In essence, this is a call to live as we were created to live from the beginning. Adam and Eve were created to live in love, but they chose not to. And their offspring have struggled ever since. Adam and Eve had two boys, Cain and Abel. Cain murdered his brother Abel because he was jealous that God thought more highly of Abel's offerings to God. Cain murdered his brother because he was selfishly self-focused.

The law was given to man by God as an instruction to refrain from what was self-focused. If mankind had been loving, mankind would not have needed the law, for love fulfills the law.

Love does no wrong to a neighbor. Therefore love is the fulfillment of the law. Romans 13:10 (NET)

This is a very short study on love, but it should be apparent that being self-focused (selfish) and prideful is opposed to being loving and humble. A self-focus takes a view that life revolves around my needs and wants and desires and priorities. Whenever anything happens in life to oppose what I want or think I deserve, I get upset. This lack of love brings me down to a lowly state of pouting and proclaiming that I am not loved by God or others and that I deserve more.

Self-Focus Can Produce Self-Pity

This brings us back to the initial statements. A spoiled child is never content and happy. He is forever crying and complaining over being mistreated, shortchanged, neglected, misunderstood, not included, not getting what he wants and anything else with the intent of expecting to be treated as "number one".

That is his attitude in normal circumstances. Now consider his attitude when real hardship comes along in his life. It does not have to be extreme. It may be as simple as a mother who has several small children. She began her marriage with few responsibilities, but now she is required to be a continuous servant to her young children. She has to give up her freedom to do and go wherever and whenever she wants. She is tied down to the needs and cares of her children. Much of her day is consumed with tedious tasks of cooking, cleaning, changing diapers, bathing and any other routine daily chores, not to mention that she is on-call day and night. Being a mother is a high calling of God. It is an opportunity to not only bring a new human being into this life, but also to nurture, train, love and encourage her children in order to bring them to maturity in Jesus Christ as adults. It is a God-given opportunity to raise a child for God, to bring about his glory and purposes on earth. But this high calling cannot be met when we are rebellious. And a self-focused attitude will rob its victim of appreciation and thankfulness. The victim will feel trapped without hope of escape. And depression will set in. This mother needs encouragement for sure. But the root of her depression is an attitude of living for self, and an unwillingness to live for her children and God.

We can endure all sorts of hardships if our attitude is rightly focused. A self-focused attitude will not bring about freedom. Thankfulness is evidence of having a right focus of our lives.

I have sat with many men in my routine work years. It is commonplace to find them complaining about everything possible. They complain about supervision and the company. They complain about fellow workers. They complain about their wives and children. They complain about anyone in authority. They blame someone for every difficulty, every problem and anything that does not conform to their own opinions and desires. These complainers certainly don't appear happy and content. Depressed, self-focused people are not content with their lives. They are not thankful—all they can see is the negative. And the negative is exaggerated, while the blessings in their lives are overlooked. They don't know God! God is our life and our future, but only if we truly know him.

The Self-Focused Pursuit of Affirmation

Many have been raised in controlling households. The control may have come in the form of criticism, judgment, excessive rules and a lack of freedom to be who we are. Every parent and household must have standards and principles which they live by. And these standards and principles must be observed and enforced. For example, it is not unreasonable or controlling for a father to expect that his children will not swear in the home, or to smoke, or to use drugs, or to use pornography and many other ungodly behaviors.

So what constitutes a controlling father or mother? It occurs mainly when the enforcement of certain behaviors lack love and encouragement. It is clearly possible to have too many rules in a home, but even in these homes, if love, appreciation, affirmation and encouragement are poured out in abundance, most any child will feel secure and free to be themselves.

Unfortunately, parents who are controllers are more likely to be judgmental and critical rather than encouraging, loving, appreciative and affirming. Children raised in these controlling environments that lack the assurance that they are loved and valuable in the eyes of those in authority over them will likely struggle with feeling good about themselves. And they will also fear and reject having someone in authority over them. In childhood, their experience had been that those in authority abused who they were by their critical control. They were not free to be themselves, and they were not valued by those in authority. So now, in their adult years, they reject being subject to those in authority. In fact, they may find that they are now the ones who are driven to be in control—in authority. If they are in control, they won't have to submit to someone else's control. These people are driven by fear, by pride and by rebellion. They fear the judgments of others. They see themselves as the one who is the best judge, and their security is based on being the judge. After all, who can judge the judge? This is a foundation of pride. In reality, everyone must submit to authority in some place or fashion. We are instructed to submit to one another. (Ephesians 5:21) We are called to become servants, as Jesus became a servant. We are to have his attitude. (Philippians 2:3-8) This is critical for us to bond together and to function as one. But those who must be in control and who do not submit to others find it nearly impossible to walk as one with others.

These people find themselves isolated from others. Ironically, their basic need to be affirmed and united with others—which was missing in their childhood years—is now missing in their adult years. This time it is not because those in authority are mistreating them; rather, it is because they have set themselves apart from others and have established themselves as not willing to submit to others, and, at the same time, expecting to be the one in control. And they see those who do not submit to their control as rejecting them as a person. They need loving affirmation from those in authority, but they have established themselves as being over others and reject being subject to authority. Now the affirmation they crave will never come.

It gets worse. Affirmation can also come from our peers or from those who are subject to our authority, such as our employees, our children or anyone who is in a place of service to us. But people who are controllers themselves do not affirm others out of love. And those who are under their control feel the lack of affirmation and freedom to be who they truly are. They are not lifted up, but manipulated and pushed down through judgment and criticism. It is not likely that these abused subjects will affirm the one over them—the one who oppresses them. So now the prideful, controlling person is left all alone. He is a setup for depression because he is void of his basic need for loving affirmation. Ironically, in his desperation for affirmation he has set himself above others, thinking that now he is in control of affirmation since he is in a place of authority. But in all of his struggles to become affirmed, affirmation never comes.

This whole scenario is filled with irony. If he really wants loving affirmation from those around him, the best way to get it is to lovingly affirm others. And the best way to receive affirmation from those in authority is to submit to authority, to take the place of a servant, not expecting to be the one who is honored and served. And the best way to be affirmed and honored by our peers is to raise them up.

People who suffer from a lack of affirmation and have become controllers themselves and who do not submit to others are spiritual cripples inside. They need healing from within. And how do they heal? First, they need to recognize and confess their own sinful, prideful and controlling behavior. Second, choose to repent. Begin to lower yourself and to submit to others. Everyone is under authority, even Jesus. (1 Corinthians 11:3, 15:24-28) Come to understand your rebellion, and then submit to others. *Don't be fooled into thinking that you don't have to submit to others because you submit to God. It is God who commands us to submit to one another out of reverence to God.* (Ephesians 5:21) Thirdly, affirm others. Raise others up by lowering yourself down and becoming their servant. Fourthly, look to Jesus and your heavenly Father for your affirmation. And your affirmation will come as you obediently die to self and serve your God. The prideful will never be affirmed! Obediently walk in these steps, and you will find joy from within. Do not give way to fear. (1 Peter 3:5-6, 1 John 4:18) Depression will lose its grip on you.

Not everyone who grew up in a controlling family will become a controller themselves as an adult. Many go in the opposite direction; they become pleasers. They are in such fear of losing affirmation from others that they do whatever others seem to want. They are forever apologizing and giving in to the wishes of others. The hope is that they will be affirmed because they give everyone what they want. Unfortunately, they still do not receive the affirmation they crave. If they give in to every demand of their own children, their children will become spoiled cry babies. They will not become thankful and appreciative; rather, they will become unthankful complainers.

In addition, as the pleaser gives in to everyone else's wishes, they find that they have depleted themselves of any personal satisfaction. They are drained, not filled. They are frustrated, not at peace. They are burned out inside by endlessly trying to please others at the expense of their own being. At this point, they don't even know who they are because they have not been living out their true self in the face of others. This is a very lonely existence. Even though they appear to have been loving and pleasant, inside they have been driven to be in control of the affirmation from others, but the affirmation is never a reality. This whole way of relating to others is phony and leaves one empty inside. The consequence is not the affirmation pursued, but frustration and hopelessness. The pleaser appears very sociable, pleasant and connected with people, but inside they are isolated and alone. Inside they struggle with frustration, loneliness and depression.

Being a pleaser is not the same as being one who loves others. The outward actions may appear loving, but the inward motives are quite different. Love is driven out of a decision to give of ourselves so that others will receive a blessing. A pleaser is driven out of a need for affirmation and the fear of being rejected. For example, pleasers may spoil their children with the intent of receiving their loving appreciation. In contrast, loving parents will intentionally discipline and withhold what they demand in order to develop godly character in their children.

There is an irony with the pleaser as there is with the controller. In the example of their children, being a pleaser never results in thankful affirmation. However, the one who lovingly disciplines and withholds finds that his/her children become thankful and appreciative of others, including their parents.

The deliverance from depression for the controller or the pleaser is the same. Repent of your self-focused behavior and seek God's wisdom to truly know yourself. Controllers and pleasers do not know themselves; they are driven without understanding their own motives. Having godly motives as inspired by the Spirit brings transformation. And then, when we obediently follow the direction of the Spirit for a new way of living, we find that affirmation comes from God. This is our true, lasting, functional and foundational hope. Depression loses its foundation to the foundation of the Spirit.

A Focus on God's Will and Purpose in Our Suffering

Living in the understanding of God's will before our will is an attitude that opposes depression. This is even true when we are subject to suffering that is legitimately severe. Maybe you have a crippling disease. Maybe you are subject to frequent or continuous pain. Maybe you lost a loved one in a car accident or to a serious illness. Maybe you were fired from your job. These are all circumstances of real and severe situations that bring real and severe suffering. But even—especially—in these circumstances, we need to draw near to God and live for him. Suffering can draw our attention to ourselves, but it can also draw our attention to God. It is a choice to become self-focused, seeking our own will, or to become God-focused in order to fulfill God's will. Think of the suffering of Jesus in the garden just before being ridiculed, tortured and murdered on a cross. His torment in the garden was not worry and fear of what was about to happen. His suffering was the burden of the sins of all mankind. The Scriptures tell us that he was about to die right there in the garden due to the stress upon his body. The anguish was so intense that he sweat drops of blood. Suffering could not have been more intense, yet Jesus' focus was on the will of God. (Luke 22:41-44, Matthew 26:38-42) After he prayed, the angels came to strengthen him, so he continued to pray. He did not die there in the garden. He was strengthened by the angels so that he could go on to be ridiculed, tortured and hung on a cross to die. Jesus focused on his Father's will before his own will.

> Going a little farther, he fell with his face to the ground and prayed, "My Father, if it is possible, may this cup be taken from me. Yet not as I will, but as you will." Matthew 26:39 (NIV)

Jesus did not have to understand everything in order to give up his life. It did not have to make sense. Dying, suffering, loss and rejection can seem very purposeless. But faith trusts God that he has a purpose, even if we do not understand it. His will is to be done, whether we are privileged to know why he does what he does or not. We are to trust and obey with the hope and faith that God loves us and is accomplishing something much bigger and outside of our understanding.

Jesus endured the suffering, the rejection of mankind, the ridicule and torture, and even the excruciating death on a cross by keeping his focus on God's purposes and God's promises. He focused on what God was doing through his life and the final outcome. Having a right-focus is critically foundational in the midst of suffering. We are admonished to have the same view of our suffering.

> Therefore, since we are surrounded by so great a cloud of witnesses, let us also lay aside every weight, and sin which clings so closely, and let us run with endurance the race that is set before us, looking to Jesus, the founder and perfecter of our faith, **who for the joy that was set before him endured the cross, despising the shame, and is seated at the right hand of the throne of God**. Consider him who endured from sinners such hostility against himself, so that you may not grow weary or fainthearted. In your struggle against sin you have not yet resisted to the point of shedding your blood. Hebrews 12:1-4 (ESV)

Read chapter eleven of Hebrews to discover this "great cloud of witnesses" referred in this passage. They all suffered intensely. Some were tortured, mocked, flogged, imprisoned, stoned, stabbed, killed and even sawn in two. They suffered for Christ and held to their convictions because they kept their eyes focused on Christ and the promise of being united with him for eternity. Jesus is our ultimate example.

Okay, we are not Jesus. We are not the Son of God. But Jesus was a man just like each of us. He needed the angels to strengthen him. He needed to pray to his heavenly Father for strength. In this respect, we are no different. Jesus also had the Spirit of God living within him. But after his resurrection, he sent this same Spirit to live within each one of us who have been born again by his Spirit. We are now like him.

Attitude and perspective are everything. It determines our state of being and how we are to live. You may have heard of Elizabeth Elliot (1926-2015). She was the wife of Jim Elliot. Both Jim and Elizabeth knew that they were called to become Jesus' missionaries. They met in college, fell in love, but did not marry for five and a half years as they waited upon the Lord's will. They did not want their wills to interfere with God's will for their lives.

In 1953 they were married in Ecuador and proceeded together to befriend an unreached, violent and isolated tribal people in the rain forests of eastern Ecuador, the Auca Indians. In just over two years of marriage, living in the jungle, Elizabeth's husband and four other missionaries landed their plane on the river shores of the Aucas. They tried to befriend them, but the Indians speared all five of them to death.

Elizabeth stayed on with the other widowed wives. She finished translating the Bible into their language, and along with the other widows, befriended these natives and led the men who killed their husbands to Christ. These women endured many hardships, but their main focus was God's will, not their own.

Elizabeth faced many painful disappointments, but she continued on with Christ. In the midst of her translating, she had another native who helped her, but he was murdered before she finished. She had three years of translation notes in a suitcase that were transported on the top of a banana truck. Her suitcase was stolen, along with her tedious years of work. But Elizabeth did not lose focus. God knew, and God was in control. She gave up her will to his. She gave up her life to God to use as he saw fit.

She remained single for about eight years and remarried in 1963, but after four years, lost her second husband to cancer. About four years later, she married again. Her life finished its course with ten years of mini-strokes and dementia.

Elisabeth Elliot endured a victorious life of struggles. She viewed life as a life with God, a life for God and by God. She made many strong statements about how to live for Christ in the midst of trials. Here are a few:

God's ways are mysterious and our faith develops strong muscles as we negotiate the twists and turns of our lives.
—*The Elisabeth Elliot Newsletter*, November/December, 2003

The secret is Christ in me, not me in a different set of circumstances.
— Elisabeth Elliot, *Keep a Quiet Heart*

To be a follower of the Crucified means, sooner or later, a personal encounter with the cross. And the cross always entails loss. The great symbol of Christianity means sacrifice and no one who calls himself a Christian can evade this stark fact.
— Elisabeth Elliot, *These Strange Ashes*

I realized that the deepest spiritual lessons are not learned by His letting us have our way in the end, but by His making us wait, bearing with us in love and patience until we are able to honestly pray what He taught His disciples to pray: Thy will be done.
— Elisabeth Elliot, *Passion and Purity: Learning to Bring Your Love Life Under Christ's Control*

She gives us a simple understanding of what it means to become a follower of Jesus Christ.

Trust Him! Do what he says!
—Elisabeth Elliot, *Quest for Love, pg. 134*

Her husband wrote,

> "He is no fool who gives what he cannot keep to gain that which he cannot lose." Jim Elliot, missionary to Auca indians in Ecuador"
> — Elisabeth Elliot, *The Journals of Jim Elliot*

It is easy to complain about our suffering. The Elliot's embraced it. And it is all to the glory of God. God does not exist for our will and our purposes; we exist for his. Jesus taught us to pray, "Your kingdom come. Your will be done on earth as it is in heaven." (Matthew 6:10) This is easy to pray, but much more difficult to live out when in the midst of suffering, setbacks and loss. Needless to say, God's purposes will prevail, in spite of our attitudes or view of our lives. *This conflict of attitudes and views will only bring about confusion, doubt and despair. Peace comes from aligning our view of our lives with God's purposes. Depression comes from a lack of hope, a lack of purpose for our suffering, a lack of unity with God and a failure to escape God's will by any of our own efforts. Peace comes when we surrender our will to God's will—when we trust him with our lives because he is a loving God with a much larger purpose and perspective of all things than our minute ability to understand.*

It might be good for us to rephrase the Lord's prayer to make it more personal: "Your kingdom come in and through my life. Your will, not my will, be done in my life as it is in heaven and needs to be in my life here on earth."

David knew what it was like to be pursued by enemies. He was frequently on the run from Saul. One time, as he hid in a cave to hide from Saul, who sought after him to kill him, he cried out to the Lord. But not for his will to be done, but that God's purposes would be fulfilled in David.

> I cry out to God Most High, to God who fulfills his purpose for me.
> Psalm 57:2 (ESV)

In another Psalm David professes again that the Lord will fulfill his purposes in his life. Even though David endured many conflicts throughout his life, he saw God's loving hand upon him because he was part of God's purposes. He knew that he was a living tool in the hands of God to fulfill God's work. And David implores God not to remove his hand upon his life. David desired to be used by God for God's purposes, even when it was very difficult.

> Though I walk in the midst of trouble, you preserve my life; you stretch out your hand against the wrath of my enemies, and your right hand delivers me. The LORD will fulfill his purpose for me; your steadfast love, O LORD, endures forever. Do not forsake the work of your hands. Psalm 138:7-8 (ESV)

Man has many plans and purposes of his own. Because of the fall of man, we live our lives apart from God, seeking our own will. Much of the time we are fighting against God by seeking our will instead of his will. Ironically, we even may call out to him to grant us our will. And it is not wrong for us to call out to him for deliverance, healing, protection, provision or anything that we may need. But there comes a point when we must surrender our will to his will. We must rest in his life for us and stop struggling to change his will to have it conform to ours. We are God's creation for his work and purposes, and that is how it is going to be.

> Many are the plans in the mind of a man, but it is the purpose of the LORD that will stand. Proverbs 19:21 (ESV)

Jesus made a promise to us. It was a conditional promise. He said that if we would just seek his kingdom and his righteousness that all the things that the world strives after would be given to us as well. (Matthew 6:33) I don't think that he meant we would all become rich and that everything would be without suffering and trials. He also said that in order to follow him that we had to be willing to face suffering, similar to his suffering on the cross. He also said that in order to save our lives we had to lose our lives for his purposes at the expense of living for our own purposes.

> Then he said to them all: "If anyone would come after me, he must **deny himself and take up his cross daily** and follow me. For whoever wants to save his life will lose it, but whoever loses his life for me will save it. What good is it for a man to gain the whole world, and yet lose or forfeit his very self? Luke 9:23-25 (NIV)

David understood his relationship with God was one of living to do his Lord's will for his Lord's name's sake. He asked God to teach him to do his will.

> **Teach me to do your will, for you are my God**; may your good Spirit lead me on level ground. **For your name's sake, O LORD**, preserve my life; in your righteousness, bring me out of trouble. Psalm 143:10-11 (NIV)

When we call God by the name of "Lord", we are acknowledging that he is the master over all things, particularly over our lives. We live to do his will, whatever that may cost us. Our eternal inheritance is a matter of being conformed into the likeness of Christ so that we can fulfill God's will in his kingdom forever. That is our eternal inheritance. God loves us, but we were created to live for him and his purposes.

> In him we have obtained an inheritance, having been predestined **according to the purpose of him who works all things according to the counsel of his will**, so that we who were the first to hope in Christ might be to the praise of his glory. Ephesians 1:11-12 (ESV)

Depression comes when we fight against God's will for us. Peace and joy come when we unify our lives with God by resting in what God is doing in and through us for his eternal purposes.

Reflection Questions

Describe how or where you are selfishly independent of God. In other words, how do you live as though you are self-reliant, not needing God?

Describe how you are self-focused (selfish) and prideful versus being loving and humble. How has your love for someone else been your inner strength? How have you planted the seeds of depression by complaining that someone has done you wrong?

How do you complain about how your needs and wants are not being met? What do you pout about, as though God or others do not love you as you think they should?

Do you see your life as belonging to yourself, or to God? When God brings suffering and hardship into your life, what is your attitude? Do you obediently serve him, and rejoice in his purposes for you?

Chapter 4

The Joy of the Lord

Depression is a state of loss, of anxiety, of frustration, of spiritual pain—a state with no future hope. Joy is the opposite of depression. Joy is a state of peace, comfort and anticipation based on a hope in the future. It is a state of being optimistic versus pessimistic about what lies ahead in life. But how can we have a hope in the future? No one has control over what is going to happen. Sure, we can make our plans to get married, go to college, start a career, save money to buy a house and many other dreams and aspirations. We can make these plans, and to some extent we can make them happen. But reality frequently reveals that the future will bring things into our lives that we never desired or anticipated. Reality reveals how little control we have over what comes into our lives.

> Consider what God has done: Who can straighten what he has made crooked? When times are good, be happy; but when times are bad, consider: God has made the one as well as the other. Therefore, a man cannot discover anything about his future. Ecclesiastes 7:13-14 (NIV)

If we ponder this truth, we will find many examples in nearly every life we know. Everyone experiences unplanned and unwanted circumstances. For example, whoever marries expecting painful conflict and divorce? Yet there is one divorce for every two marriages across our country. Or, who expects their house to become repossessed? Reports vary, but about 5 to 8 million families have experienced a home foreclosure since 2007. I suspect that most of those families joyfully moved into their new house when they purchased it with the expectation of living there until they decided to move. But then the housing market fell when these "owners" discovered they could not pay back their loans. The stock market took a great plunge as well, and many who were planning on early retirement were faced with working much longer—if not already too late. Or, who expects to have a serious illness? Why has medical insurance been such a big deal? We all need our health, and we can forgo many health problems if we are diligent about taking responsible care for our health. But some problems just happen and are unavoidable. Our daughter was diagnosed with leukemia when she was ten years old and went on two and a half years of chemotherapy. She is now twenty-four and healthy. We are thankful for the medical technology developments. We are thankful for the chemotherapy advancements over the past fifty years. If this had happened twenty years earlier, we most likely would have lost her.

These kinds of examples are real and all about us. And for the most part, we cannot prevent them. Our ability to control our future is miniscule.

Pride lies to us. It convinces us that we are in control and that we can determine the outcomes of tomorrow. But reality proves that the prideful do not own tomorrow. James implores us to wake up to the truth about all of our self-empowered plans.

> Come now, you who say, "Today or tomorrow we will go into this or that town and spend a year there and do business and make a profit." You do not know about tomorrow. What is your life like? For you are a puff of smoke that appears for a short time and then vanishes. You ought to say instead, "If the Lord is willing, then we will live and do this or that." But as it is, you boast in your arrogance. All such boasting is evil. James 4:13-16 (NET)

Depression sets in when we make our plans, but our plans do not work out. And possibly get worse instead—loss, disappointment, struggles and pain come into our lives. The sudden reality that we cannot control the future outcomes overwhelms us, and depression sets in.

So is there no such thing as a true hope for the future, one based on truth and reality? This can only be so if our hope is in someone who has full and ultimate control of the future. And this person must also love me and have my future in best regards. Who puts their hopes in a powerless, evil or hateful person? We put our hope in someone who loves us. We put our hope in someone who has the power and authority to fulfill his promises.

A little child puts his hope in his father and mother, assuming that he has loving, stable and responsible parents. A five year old who has a good home does not worry about tomorrow. He does not concern himself with his future. He just naturally assumes that his parents are handling his needs for food, clothing, shelter and protection. He looks to his parents to make all life decisions. He trusts them with his life. He trusts them because they love him and have his needs as a priority in their lives. They will even sacrifice of their own freedoms and needs in order to care for him. He also knows that he is small and they are big. He realizes that he knows about some things, but he is just learning. But his parents—they know everything, and can do everything. (At least, that is how he perceives it.) And he doesn't worry about being alone; he has a family. He may go out to play, but he always comes home to a warm, loving and safe place, his family—headed by his father and mother. He is secure and happy.

I know that many did not grow up in such secure and loving homes as described. I also know that homes like this are becoming rare as our society has lost touch with the family structure as God created it to be from the beginning. Forty-two percent of our children are born out-of-wedlock. And half of all our children have experienced the divorce of their parents. And the stay-home mom is becoming a thing of the past. Most kids are latch-key kids, coming home from school to find and empty house. Families are not what they used to be. Parents are not what they used to be. People are not what they used to be. Our culture is filled with distractions and deceptions that have ruined the wholesome family structure that is mostly a memory from ages past.

Now the children who grew up in unstable and unloving homes have become adults. Their childhood was probably depressing, and their own struggle with depression has its roots from those childhood years. Now they are adults, maybe with their own dysfunctional homes and lifestyles. No wonder that so many struggle with depression today.

Where can we find hope when we live in such a depressing society with so little to stand upon for security and love? There is only one who can give us that assurance—the almighty, living and eternal God who created all things, the one who has authority over all that exists, including the future. He is a god of love. In fact, his word tells us that "God is love." (1 John 4:8 & 16) All loves finds it source in God. Our love for one another is actually God's love flowing from God through each one of us to another. God is a river of life, a river of love. (Revelation 22:1-2) We are all struggling for life, but Jesus defines life; Jesus is life—eternal life. And he desires for us to have his life. Jesus sent his Spirit for us as a spring of the water of life that would continually flow from within us. (John 4:13-14, Revelation 21:6) God is our heavenly Father in whom we can trust as a little child puts his trust in his loving and strong earthly father.

> See how very much our Father loves us, for he calls us his children, and that is what we are! But the people who belong to this world don't recognize that we are God's children because they don't know him. 1 John 3:1 (NLT)

Not everyone is a child of God. As this verse states, the children of the world do not recognize the children of God. We become children of God by being born into his family. We become born again by the Spirit of God, whom he freely gives to all who ask. (John 3:3-8) Those who have the Spirit of God are children of God. (Romans 8:9, 13-17) We all have had sinful fathers. Some have loved us to some degree. Many have been abusive. But our heavenly Father is a perfect father of love and care. And he promises to pour out his Spirit to anyone who calls out to him. This is a hope that we can stand upon.

If you then, although you are evil, know how to give good gifts to your children, how much more will the heavenly Father give the Holy Spirit to those who ask him!" Luke 11:13 (NET)

This is a hope that we can trust in, the love of our Creator, our heavenly Father who gives us his own Spirit to reside within us as we live out our journey in this troubled world.

We know how much God loves us, and we have put our trust in his love. God is love, and all who live in love live in God, and God lives in them. 1 John 4:16 (NLT)

I have a good friend, James, who is in prison serving a life sentence. His life had been filled with drugs and crime. When first sentenced, he found himself all alone in a county jail prison cell with no hope of getting out and having a normal life on the outside. Depression overwhelmed him and all he wanted was to die and get it over with. He called out to God to kill him; he just wanted to die. To his surprise, he heard God tell him to get lower. He got to his knees. Then he heard that he needed to get lower, so he got on his hands and knees. Then he heard to get lower, so he laid down prostrate. Then, as the Spirit enabled, he began to confess all of his sins. This went on for more than an hour. He then found himself on his feet with hands raised praising the Lord as the Spirit spoke through his lips. James called out to God for death, and God answered his prayer. The old James was crucified and a new James rose from the floor. God filled him with Life. He had been filled with the Holy Spirit. And his life has never been the same. The old James lays dead on the county jail prison floor. The new James is joyful and fully alive, even as he spends each and every day in prison. In his depression he called out to God, and God answered him.

When we are in the midst of our struggle of despairing depression, we need to call out to God as James had done. At this point, we only have one hope, and that hope resides in God Almighty.

Why am I so depressed? Why this turmoil within me? Put your hope in God, for I will still praise Him, my Savior and my God. Psalm 42:5 (HCSB)

Pure Joy in the Face of Suffering

Putting our hope in God does not assure us that we will not face painful trials. This life was destined for frustration from the day that Adam and Eve decided to try to live out their lives on their own apart from the wise counsel of God. We all live in that fallen state, whether we believe in God or not. As Christians, our ultimate hope is in the future when we will be delivered from this fallen state in which we all live.

> **I consider that our present sufferings are not worth comparing with the glory that will be revealed in us**. The creation waits in eager expectation for the sons of God to be revealed. For the creation was subjected to frustration, not by its own choice, but by the will of the one who subjected it, **in hope that the creation itself will be liberated from its bondage to decay and brought into the glorious freedom of the children of God**.
> We know that the whole creation has been groaning as in the pains of childbirth right up to the present time. Not only so, but we ourselves, who have the firstfruits of the Spirit, groan inwardly as we wait eagerly for our adoption as sons, the redemption of our bodies. **For in this hope we were saved. But hope that is seen is no hope at all. Who hopes for what he already has? But if we hope for what we do not yet have, we wait for it patiently**. Romans 8:18-25 (NIV)

True joy is based on true hope. And the only true hope available to anyone is a hope in God's love for his creation, and especially mankind, whom he created to be like him in his image. The day is coming when he will restore those who trust in him and, in faith, seek him now. Notice that this passage says that "in this hope we were saved". And "Who hopes for what he already has?" This is a hope that sustains our joy in the midst of life's many trials. It is dependent upon God's promises for those who love him. It is a joy that proceeds from our faith in the one who holds the future of all that exists. It is a faith in his faithfulness to his promises for all who are his own and who love him. It is a joy that exists in the midst of painful struggles.

Struggles Can Be a Source for Joy

No one looks forward to struggles and hardship. We don't plan them into our lives; they just happen. Victory comes from our viewpoint of and attitude toward these struggles when they occur. We can even find joy in the midst of our struggles with the right attitude. Does God deliver us from struggles? Absolutely! But just as he may deliver us, he may also subject us to struggles for our own spiritual formation. *Struggles may be hard on us, but good for us.* Understanding the good that can come out of our struggles is a source for pure joy. Consider James and Paul's words on suffering and the good that comes from our trials.

> Consider it pure joy, my brothers, whenever you face trials of many kinds, because you know that the testing of your faith develops perseverance. Perseverance must finish its work so that you may be mature and complete, not lacking anything. James 1:2-4 (NIV)

> Not only this, but we also rejoice in sufferings, knowing that suffering produces endurance, and endurance, character, and character, hope. And hope does not disappoint, because the love of God has been poured out in our hearts through the Holy Spirit who was given to us. Romans 5:3-5 (NET)

I ran the quarter mile on our high school track team. Training for this event meant repetitively running half this distance (220 yards) at a specified time. The coach had me run one after another. I would run one, jog for two minutes to catch my breath, and then he would have me run another. I would be on the track after everyone else went for the locker room shower. I complained, "Coach, everyone else has gone in; why are you keeping me out here?" And he would reply, "You're still hitting the times; get back on the track." These repetitive 220 yard runs were painful and exhausting. Why did the coach do this to me? He wanted me to be fast. He wanted me to be a winner. And I became both fast and a winner. My coach loved me.

Our heavenly Father loves us. He is our coach. The Spirit he gave us is called our Counselor who teaches us. (John 14:26, 15:26) God wants us to be strong and a winner in life. He wants us to be effective for him in the working of his kingdom. In our suffering, we increase our endurance to press on in this life. Our faith becomes strong. Our relationship with God becomes deep and full of purpose. And out of these difficult experiences we receive hope, because we have walked with God in his strength in the midst of our struggles.

This is not exactly what we dream of when we strive for joy. We think of joy as everything being pleasant. But as long as we hold onto this expectation, we will rob ourselves of joy. The suffering may come anyway, and because of a bad attitude or because we do not see what God is doing in us or through us, we not only suffer, but we suffer with depression rather than in the joy of knowing that God loves us and is transforming us.

We don't always see the good purpose of our suffering. So we have to trust that God knows what he is doing. The suffering may be for our refinement, but it may also be so that God can fulfill something that he is doing, and we cannot see it. Consider the sufferings of Job. He did not know what God was doing in his dealings with Satan. Sometimes our suffering is for the sake of others. Each life is connected with many other people. When we suffer, others are affected in some way.

I think of my father-in-law, who cared for his wife with Alzheimer for several years before it took her life. They were both elderly at the time, but he carried her burden just the same out of his committed love for her. In his mind, he just loved her as his wife. But he did such a good job of it that those around him took notice. His love brought glory to God. And he was a good role model for those who witnessed how he loved his wife to the end. He was a testimony.

I think of my dad's cousin Helen and her husband Art. Art slowly became crippled with arthritis, starting when he was in his forties. Helen was a very godly woman. She cared for him for thirty years as he became increasingly lame. In the last few years he had his legs amputated and he became blind. But she cared for him joyfully up till his last days. I remember her joy.

Art suffered for thirty years. He loved to play the piano, but as his arthritis consumed his joints, he had to give up the playing that he loved so much. He had a house on a lake and enjoyed taking his boat out on the water. But he had to give that up also. His last thirty years were ones of giving up one more thing after another, and adding one more painful affliction after another. In the last few years he couldn't walk, see, feed himself, shave, bath or any of the normal things of life. But one thing he never lost—his joy. I always remember Art's joy. I never heard him complain, and he always smiled and laughed with a pleasant joy.

Both Helen and Art were filled with joy, and it radiated from their marriage. Their marriage was a testimony to us all. They were Christians, and Jesus shined through them.

During these years, Helen also took in her aged mother and cared for her until her death. She also looked after her brother, who suffered from a genetic disease and died young.

When Art died, Helen, then in her late seventies, continued her loving service to those less capable than her. From her seventies into her eighties, she spent her time and energy caring for other elderly people in her church. Helen was a child of God. Helen passed onto her Lord at ninety-six after suffering dementia for several years. I know today that she is fully restored and in the glorious presence of her Lord, whom she served her entire life.

We live in a fallen world. Suffering is part of it. But, in spite of man's disobedient rejection of God, God has not abandoned man. There will be a day when he will fully redeem his creation, and all suffering will disappear.

And I heard a loud voice from the throne saying, "Behold, the dwelling place of God is with man. He will dwell with them, and they will be his people, and God himself will be with them as their God. He will wipe away every tear from their eyes, and death shall be no more, neither shall there be mourning, nor crying, nor pain anymore, for the former things have passed away." Revelation 21:3-4 (ESV)

We have a hope in our future with God, but that is not our only hope. We can call out to God now in our suffering and anxieties.

Humble yourselves, therefore, under God's mighty hand, that he may lift you up in due time. Cast all your anxiety on him because he cares for you. 1 Peter 5:6-7 (NIV)

We are not promised that he will deliver us from all suffering in this life, but we can count on him for comfort and joy in the midst of our suffering. Our joy is not because we enjoy the suffering, but that we are chosen by God. We are being transformed into his likeness, and we await the day of our complete salvation from the depravity of this fallen world. And while we wait, we wait with the presence of his Spirit living within us, the Spirit of joy. This is our hope and source of joy.

Blessed be the God and Father of our Lord Jesus Christ! By his great mercy **he gave us new birth into a living hope** through the resurrection of Jesus Christ from the dead, that is, into an inheritance imperishable, undefiled, and unfading. It is reserved in heaven for you, who by God's power are protected through faith for a salvation ready to be revealed in the last time. **This brings you great joy**, although you may have to suffer for a short time in various trials. Such trials show the proven character of your faith, which is much more valuable than gold—gold that is tested by fire, even though it is passing away—and will bring praise and glory and honor when Jesus Christ is revealed. You have not seen him, but you love him. You do not see him now but you believe in him, **and so you rejoice with an indescribable and glorious joy, because you are attaining the goal of your faith—the salvation of your souls.** 1 Peter 1:3-9 (NET)

Reflection Questions

What are you suffering now in your life? What anxieties are you enduring? How have you strived to overcome your situation, and how has your failure to deliver yourself robed you of joy?

How have you put your hope in the things of this world? Consider things such as drugs, money, possessions, power, people, skills and talents, or anything other than God? How much control have you had over your future?

How has God been your hope? What specifically are you hoping from him? What is your future hope in God.

How have you been able to experience joy in the midst of your struggles? How has he comforted you?

How have your hardships been good for you? How have they molded you?

How does your future hope in the salvation of your soul, and your eternal life in the kingdom of God affect your joy now in your present life?

Chapter 5

The Secret to Having Joy

As discussed in the previous chapter, it can be a battle to maintain our joy in the midst of suffering. It requires a right attitude toward our life of suffering, a right perspective of our suffering and a hope that is beyond our suffering. But many are depressed in this life with no apparent or significant suffering. They just lack joy and are consumed with depression. What can be done to promote joy?

The Bible frequently talks about sowing. This is an agrarian concept. Most of us are not farmers, but most of us have planted a garden, and at least understand the principle. If you want tomatoes, you have to plant tomato seeds. You can't just go out to the yard and expect tomatoes if you have not planted them beforehand. The same is true for the things of God, and especially the fruit of the Spirit.

> But the fruit of the Spirit is love, joy, peace, patience, kindness, goodness, faithfulness, gentleness, self-control; against such things there is no law. Galatians 5:22-23 (ESV)

The fruit of the Spirit doesn't just appear on its own; it has to be sown. We cannot sow tomato plants unless we have tomato seeds. But once we have them, we still have to plant and nurture them. The same is true for the fruit of the Spirit. Receiving the Spirit freely from God is like receiving seed to plant, but unless we plant the seeds, we will not bear the fruit.

Don't be misled—you cannot mock the justice of God. **You will always harvest what you plant.** Those who live only to satisfy their own sinful nature will harvest decay and death from that sinful nature. But **those who live to please the Spirit will harvest everlasting life from the Spirit**. So let's not get tired of doing what is good. At just the right time we will reap a harvest of blessing if we don't give up. Therefore, whenever we have the opportunity, we should do good to everyone— especially to those in the family of faith. Galatians 6:7-10 (NLT)

Notice that we are all sowing something. We can sow to our sinful nature or we can sow to the Spirit's nature. If we sow to the sinful nature, we will reap a destructive life that will likely bring about all sorts of situations for frustration, discouragement, hardship, struggles and lay a foundation for depression. Sowing to the Spirit will bring about a wholesome life that is pleasing to our soul and will bring about true riches of true life.

So why doesn't every Christian who has received the Spirit sow to the Spirit and produce this life-giving fruit? To answer this question, let's consider a familiar sowing example. When we prepare the soil to plant a garden of vegetables, we first have to pull out all of the weeds. Where did the weeds come from? Their seeds just blew in all by themselves. No one has to labor to plant weeds. Even after you have planted the vegetables, you will have to continually pull out the weeds. Weeds are in conflict with vegetables.

Sowing to the Spirit is much the same. The sinful desires of the flesh come naturally, and sowing to them comes without effort. In fact, it takes great effort to resist the desires of the sinful nature within us. They are the weeds in our lives. The weeds will strangle the vegetables and make them unfruitful. Similarly, the desires of the sinful nature are opposed to the desires of the Spirit. There is a continual conflict between them.

So I say, let the Holy Spirit guide your lives. Then you won't be doing what your sinful nature craves. The sinful nature wants to do evil, which is just the opposite of what the Spirit wants. And the Spirit gives us desires that are the opposite of what the sinful nature desires. These two forces are constantly fighting each other, so you are not free to carry out your good intentions. Galatians 5:16-17 (NLT)

It is easy and natural to go the way of the sinful nature, but we have been given the Spirit so that we can crucify the sinful nature and sow to the ways of the Spirit.

Those who live according to the sinful nature have their minds set on what that nature desires; but those who live in accordance with the Spirit have their minds set on what the Spirit desires. The mind of sinful man is death, but the mind controlled by the Spirit is life and peace; the sinful mind is hostile to God. It does not submit to God's law, nor can it do so. Those controlled by the sinful nature cannot please God.

You, however, are controlled not by the sinful nature but by the Spirit, if the Spirit of God lives in you. And if anyone does not have the Spirit of Christ, he does not belong to Christ.

Therefore, brothers, we have an obligation—but it is not to the sinful nature, to live according to it. For if you live according to the sinful nature, you will die; but if by the Spirit you put to death the misdeeds of the body, you will live, because those who are led by the Spirit of God are sons of God. Romans 8:5-9 & 12-14 (NIV)

Those who belong to Christ Jesus have crucified the sinful nature with its passions and desires. Galatians 5:24 (NIV)

Sowing is like continually pulling out the weeds, and at the same time nurturing the vegetables so that we have an abundant harvest of fruit. This is the walk of a true Christian. This is the understanding of repentance. Repentance is to stop sowing to the destructive ways of the sinful nature and to strive to sow to the ways of the Spirit. Jesus compared it to two roads. We are all traveling down one of these two.

You can enter God's Kingdom only through the narrow gate. The highway to hell is broad, and its gate is wide for the many who choose that way. But the gateway to life is very narrow and the road is difficult, and only a few ever find it. Matthew 7:13-14 (NLT)

Only Christians can sow to the Spirit because only Christians have the Spirit. But anyone who is not sowing to the Spirit by living out a fruitful life is subject to losing their joy and suffering with depression. A wayward life is depressing. A joyful life is a pursuit. We sow to it and we reap what we have sown.

The point is this: whoever sows sparingly will also reap sparingly, and whoever sows bountifully will also reap bountifully. 2 Corinthians 9:6 (ESV)

Loving Others Is the Pursuit

Many miss out on the joy of the Lord because they do not sow to reap the joy of the Lord. Joy may be part of the fruit of the Spirit, but if we do not plant the seeds of joy, we cannot expect to reap this joy. The question then becomes, how do we sow the seeds of joy?

Before answering that questions, let's take a look again at the list of the fruit of the Spirit found in Galatians 5:22-23:

love, joy, peace, patience, kindness, goodness, faithfulness, gentleness and self-control.

Love is the first one listed. Think about them; how many are dependent upon the first, to love? If we love, we will be at peace with others. If we love, we will be patient with others. If we love, we will be kind. Goodness is being like God. All that is good is from God, and God is love. (Matthew 19:17, 1 John 4:8&16) If we love, we will be faithful in our relationships. If we love others, we will be gentle with them. Sin is opposite to love. Sin offends, and without self-control, our sinful nature will reign. The fruit of the Spirit is dependent upon love as the foundation. But what about joy; how is joy related to loving others? Let's look at Jesus' words.

Just as the Father has loved me, I have also loved you; remain in my love. **If you obey my commandments, you will remain in my love**, just as I have obeyed my Father's commandments and remain in his love. I have told you these things **so that my joy may be in you, and your joy may be complete. My commandment is this—to love one another just as I have loved you**. No one has greater love than this—that one lays down his life for his friends. You are my friends if you do what I command you. John 15:9-14 (NET)

Jesus makes a very powerfully stated promise here. He said that his joy would be in us and that our joy would be complete if we would just obey his command to love one another as he loved us.

God makes many conditional promises, and this is one of them. The Psalms are filled with conditional promises, such as,

Oh, the joys of those who are kind to the poor! The LORD rescues them when they are in trouble. The LORD protects them and keeps them alive. He gives them prosperity in the land and rescues them from their enemies. The LORD nurses them when they are sick and restores them to health. Psalm 41:1-3 (NLT)

Not only do those who are kind to the poor receive joy, but the Lord also promises to rescue, to protect, to bring prosperity and good health to those who love the weak and poor. The beatitudes (Matthew 5:1-12) are a list of nine conditional promises. All of them bring about God's blessings if we will sow to the ways of God. When our lives are filled with God's blessings, we will be filled with his joy. But we must realize that this is the same principle of sowing and reaping. We sow to the ways of God, and the consequence is that we receive the blessings of God. Do you want joy?!!! Then sow to the ways of God. And the ways of God are founded on, first, loving God, and, two, loving one another. (Matthew 22:35-40) The secret to joy is to love God and to love others. Just do it and you will have joy.

The Self-Focused Do Not Find Joy

The opposite of loving others is to be self-focused. The self-focused continually look out for their own needs, wants and desires, expecting others to be blessing them, and disappointed when they don't. Jesus said that we are more blessed to give than to receive. (Acts 20:35) Blessings come to the servant, not the ones who expect to be served.

A recipe for joy is to live for the welfare of others. A recipe for depression is to live self-focused, always concerned about your own welfare, and ignoring the welfare of others.

This is not a distinction between the rich and the poor; the poor thinking that they have nothing to give. This has to do with the state of our hearts. Love comes from the heart, and so does selfishness. Anyone can love—rich or poor. Our greatest needs are not physical, at least not in the United States. Our greatest needs are relational. Most people are starving for relationships. As a consequence, most people are trying to get their share of attention from others. Most are vying for acceptance and inclusion. It is very obvious among teenagers. They will pay $50 to $100 for a pair of jeans with large holes in them (worn out) so they can look like everyone else. Adults are no different, although our means for seeking inclusion differ. We may spend enormous amounts on the right clothes, the right car, the right house or whatever defines our status. We may look to noteworthy achievements. Or we may just sulk in the painful misery of loneliness. What an irony! We struggle with acceptance and loneliness, yet we are all within reach of one another. We are all in reach of many others who struggle to be connected with other people. If so many are in need of one another, why don't we just do the obvious? We could all just fill one another's needs and we would all be fulfilled. But that is not what happens.

Instead, we suffer alone from being alone. We are all waiting for someone to notice us and reach out to engage in a relationship. And as long as we are all waiting, we will wait indefinitely. Who will be the first to break the barrier?

I have become very aware that when there is a group of people in a casual social setting, that very few actually take an interest in others. Most use their opportunity to talk about themselves. And if you are a quite person, you may go unnoticed because others are more focused on drawing attention to themselves. We have far too many strangers in the crowd—too many lonely and depressed.

One of our greatest needs is to be heard, to have someone take an interest in who we are and what we think and what is going on in our lives. But to have someone listen requires someone who is not self-focused and will love others by asking questions about them and intently listen because they want to know them. We all want to be known.

So, if you are the one who is lonely and feels like no one knows you or cares about who you are or what you think or what is going on in your life, you may also struggle with depression. The key to victory over your depression and loneliness is not to become more interesting, impressive or molded into the image of the group's criteria. The key is to become others focused. Enter into other people's lives by taking a sincere interest in who they are. Know their lives, their ambitions, their dreams, their experiences, their relationships, their struggles and feelings. Have compassion for them in their struggles. Encourage them and raise them up to become victorious in their lives. Lower yourself and become humble. Be a servant. Be a blessing. Don't be one of the self-focused in the crowd. Reach out to others, not so they will recognize you, but so that you can recognize them. *A true heartfelt servant will not likely suffer from depression. Stop focusing on yourself, and begin focusing on others. Self-focused people rarely find joy.*

There is great joy in raising others up and being able to see them doing well in life. Take the example of John. He was called by Christ to be a servant of others. His responsibility as under Jesus was to bring others into a prosperous relationship with God. And this relationship with God required that they loved one another as Jesus loved them. In other words, John sacrificed his life to bring life to others. John was a fisherman, and he gave up his livelihood to serve Christ by bringing others into a love relationship with one another. John was the one who sacrificed of his own life for others, but look at what he says about his own joy.

> **It has given me great joy** to find some of your children walking in the truth, just as the Father commanded us. And now, dear lady, I am not writing you a new command but one we have had from the beginning. **I ask that we love one another.** And this is love: that we walk in obedience to his commands. As you have heard from the beginning, **his command is that you walk in love**. 2 John 1:4-6 (NIV)

John was walking in that command, to love one another. And he experienced "great joy". This great joy is available to everyone. All that we have to do is to walk in love.

What is the ultimate key to joy? Love is imperative, but without God, there is no such thing as love. The world cannot love if the world is void of God. God is love, and God is life. There is no joy of life apart from God. Seeking God for life is the key to having life. Living a right life will bring joy to the heart.

> The law of the LORD is perfect, reviving the soul. The statutes of the LORD are trustworthy, making wise the simple. The precepts of the LORD are right, **giving joy to the heart**. The commands of the LORD are radiant, giving light to the eyes. Psalm 19:7-8 (NIV)

> The LORD strengthens and protects me; I trust in him with all my heart. I am rescued and **my heart is full of joy**; I will sing to him in gratitude. Psalm 28:7 (NET)

Reflection Questions

How are you sowing to the Spirit? How has sowing to the Spirit benefited your life? How has sowing to the sinful nature robed you of life?

What is the balance in your life between expecting or desiring others to reach into your life and love you, versus expecting yourself to reach out to others to fulfill their need to be loved and connected with others?

When you are around other people, describe your intentional acts of taking an interest in them, finding out who they are, their struggles, their interests, their experiences and dreams. Listening is good, but do you seek others out? What kinds of questions do you ask of them?

Chapter 6

Life Without Purpose

Why am I alive? What is the meaning of life? Life is filled with struggles, hardships, loss, pain, rejection—we are all just striving to survive. What is the purpose for living? What am I doing here? Why do I even exist? Do I have any purpose?

God created mankind with a need for purpose. When we lack purpose, we feel worthless. And when we feel worthless, we get depressed. Life without purpose and meaning is depressing.

We have a need for purpose. We have a need to succeed in our endeavors. And we have a need for self-worth. These are three separate needs that we all have, but all three are tied together.

Let's illustrate this with a simple example. Suppose you aspire to mechanical things, especially cars, and you like math, so you decide you want to become an engineer and work in the automobile industry. A career in this area would give you purpose in that you would develop or improve cars for all of mankind to drive. So you work hard to go to college. You graduate, and are feeling good about your success so far. You even succeed in getting a job at a major car manufacturer, and you now have a title, development engineer. Along with your purpose and success, you have a certain amount of self-worth derived from your title and occupation.

Now suppose with this new career that you have worked at a new development for a few years and have spent a considerable amount of the company's resources. You gave your superiors the hope of a few great advancements based on your work. Unfortunately, your work did not succeed. You now have spent several years working toward your goal, but you have failed. Now your job is at stake, and you may be let go (fired), and for certain, you will not get the promotion you were striving for. Now your purpose, your success and your self-worth are in serious jeopardy. You are discouraged by your failure, and you are struggling with depression.

Another example: Suppose you are a young woman. Your dream since you were a young girl was to meet a handsome man, get married and have children. You wanted to become a wife and a mother.

So you meet the handsome man and get married. You are part way there; you are now a wife. But then you find that you cannot get pregnant. You have seen all of the specialists and you have tried everything available, but you are still childless. You and your husband have discussed adoption, but he does not want to adopt, and besides, it is too expensive. You are beginning to feel less like a woman because you cannot have children. You feel like a failure to your husband and to yourself. Your dream was to become a stay-at-home mom, and now you are a bored stay-at-home wife. Furthermore, this whole letdown has affected your marriage. You both had high expectations and dreams of becoming parents and having a family, and now that seems to be impossible. So now, not only have you failed to succeed at having children, you are beginning to fail in your marriage as a wife. Your dreams for purpose as a wife and mom have failed, and you are not feeling very good about yourself. Your loss of all three needs of purpose, success and self-worth has brought you into a deep struggle with depression.

We all like to see our lives as a steady progression from one fulfillment to another. Each progression is based on some purpose in mind. Achieving these purposes gives us the satisfaction of success. And as we fulfill our purposes, we feel good about our lives and ourselves. This is not a sinfully selfish pursuit; we were created by God with a desire to pursue and to experience the fruit of our labors. We were created by God with a need to have value based on who we are and what we do.

Selfish Ambitions

Of course, like most everything in life, we can have sinful pursuits and a prideful view of ourselves. Not all ambitions are righteous. Not all ambitions are good for us. And not all ambitions, if fulfilled will give us a sense of purpose, success and self-worth. Many of our ambitions can be borne out of insecurity, self-preservation and fear. Many of our selfish ambitions serve only ourselves and no one else.

Selfish ambitions are born out of our sinful nature, and are not of the Spirit. Purposes, ambitions and self-worth are good, but we can have those that are driven by God's Spirit and have godly purposes, and bear the fruit of the Spirit. And conversely, we can have purposes, ambitions and prideful worth that are not driven by the Spirit, but by the sinful flesh. We need to know ourselves and know the difference. In terms of depression, only purposes, ambitions and self-worth that are derived by the Spirit will produce a deep and lasting satisfaction. The other is only a counterfeit that deceives us and will eventually rob us of life.

I say then, **walk by the Spirit and you will not carry out the desire of the flesh**. For **the flesh desires what is against the Spirit, and the Spirit desires what is against the flesh**; these are opposed to each other, so that you don't do what you want. But if you are led by the Spirit, you are not under the law.

Now the works of the flesh are obvious: sexual immorality, moral impurity, promiscuity, idolatry, sorcery, hatreds, strife, jealousy, outbursts of anger, **selfish ambitions**, dissensions, factions, envy, drunkenness, carousing, and anything similar. I tell you about these things in advance—as I told you before—that those who practice such things will not inherit the kingdom of God.

But the fruit of the Spirit is love, joy, peace, patience, kindness, goodness, faith, gentleness, self-control. Against such things there is no law. Now those who belong to Christ Jesus have crucified the flesh with its passions and desires. Since we live by the Spirit, we must also follow the Spirit. **We must not become conceited, provoking one another, envying one another**. Galatians 5:16-26 (HCSB)

It is good for us to have purpose. It is good for us to be ambitious. But it is sinfully evil to strive for selfish ambitions. What is the difference? What constitutes a selfish ambition versus a righteous ambition? I think the answer to this is determined from the state of our own heart. For example, suppose there are two men, both striving to become someone in authority. It may be a high position in a company, such as the CEO, or for a political position, such as senator, president or a judge. It may even be to become a pastor of a large church or to start a successful ministry. It really does not matter what endeavor is chosen, the driving force of the heart can be selfish ambition or righteous ambition.

So let's consider the difference between these two. The one who is driven by selfish ambition and wants to make a name for himself is prideful, and he wants others to think highly of him. He is partly driven by his own insecurities. He needs to be raised up by others because he is not content with his own understanding of who he is in the sight of his Creator. His motivations are self-serving. He is not a servant. In his striving to the top for top recognition, he is not concerned about the welfare of others. In fact, he may use others at the expense of their reputation and hard work. He wants all the credit and power. He does not delegate his power, but maintains his control—success is all about him! He is building a dynasty for himself, and he believes the lie that it's all possible due to his extraordinary abilities and achievements. His heart is filled with pride.

Now let's consider the other man. He has the same goal in mind. But his heart is quite the opposite. His ambition is not to make a name for himself so that he can be "worshiped". His ambition is to serve, and he sees his greatest opportunity to serve is to become a leader. He does not use other people in order to further his ambitions and position. Rather, he nurtures, supports and trains others in order to raise them up and to give them the satisfaction of sharing in a larger purpose for living together in harmony and unity. This man is motivated by love and walks in humility.

And, he will likely be more successful as one who serves, motivates and uplifts others. His workers are more likely to be servants, be united, be self-motivated and loyal to the company.

Both men may be striving for the same goal, but with completely opposite hearts—one evil, the other righteous. One has limited and shortsighted satisfaction which will eventually leave him stripped of self-worth. The other is filled with divine purpose, and has lasting joy in it. Even though he was not seeking to be raised up, he will be held in high regard by others, including God. Which one do you think may struggle with anxiety, stress, insecurity, emptiness and depression? Which one do you think will have lasting peace, security and value in himself?

Jesus is our ultimate example of the latter. He sat at the right hand of God on his throne in heaven. It does not get much higher than that. But he lowered himself down and became a servant among those whom he created. We are to be like him.

> If you have **any encouragement from being united with Christ**, if any **comfort from his love**, if any **fellowship with the Spirit**, if any tenderness and compassion, then make my joy complete by being like-minded, having the same love, being one in spirit and purpose. **Do nothing out of selfish ambition or vain conceit, but in humility consider others better than yourselves.** Each of you should look not only to your own interests, but also to the interests of others. **Your attitude should be the same as that of Christ Jesus**: Who, being in very nature God, did not consider equality with God something to be grasped, but **made himself nothing, taking the very nature of a servant**, being made in human likeness. Philippians 2:1-7 (NIV)

Jesus' disciples, James and John, were trying to use their relationship with Jesus to gain a higher place in his kingdom. They wanted to sit to his right and his left when he came in the glory of his kingdom. They wanted to be glorified by others with Jesus. The other disciples were indignant toward them.

So Jesus called them together and said, "You know that the rulers in this world lord it over their people, and officials flaunt their authority over those under them. But among you it will be different. **Whoever wants to be a leader among you must be your servant, and whoever wants to be first among you must be the slave of everyone else.** For even the Son of Man came not to be served but to serve others and to give his life as a ransom for many." Mark 10:42-45 (NLT)

Selfish ambitions do not satisfy. If you are struggling with depression, looking for purpose in life, selfish ambitions will not fill your soul with purpose. They will not put your life on a solid foundation. You will find yourself working very hard and long, but never finding the satisfaction you are striving for. It is a "chasing after the carrot". You are the donkey, and someone is riding you. They carry the stick with a carrot on it and dangle it before your face, and you never quite get what you are seeking. You will only wear yourself out in your striving, and you will never be nourished with lasting purpose and satisfaction. The devil is the one holding the stick with the carrot that you are chasing after. Jesus holds the kingdom of God in his hand, and he invites you to join him in the establishment of his kingdom. Which one do you think offers lasting satisfaction for your soul? These two ambitions are opposed to one another, and they are not mutually inclusive. We all have to choose one or the other.

Who is wise and has understanding among you? He should show his works by good conduct with wisdom's gentleness. But if you have **bitter envy and selfish ambition in your heart**, don't brag and deny the truth. Such wisdom does not come from above but is earthly, unspiritual, demonic. For **where envy and selfish ambition exist, there is disorder and every kind of evil**. But the **wisdom from above is first pure, then peace-loving, gentle, compliant, full of mercy and good fruits, without favoritism and hypocrisy**. James 3:13-17 (HCSB)

Caution: Your ambition may be a godly endeavor, such as a pastor or a Bible teacher. You may even be very good at what you do, even anointed by God. But you may still be driven by selfish ambition.

King Nebuchadnezzar's Pride

The issue is not so much what we strive after, but the purpose of our hearts in our strivings. One man can strive to become the head of his organization because he is seeking recognition, worth in the face of others, power and control. Another man can seek the same position because he is called to be a servant leader. His aim is to raise others up, to bring prosperity to his organization for the welfare of others and to lead the organization in a godly direction that brings glory to God. These are two men who are seeking the same position, but with very opposite states of their hearts intent. Which one do you think will be most content, at peace and satisfied in life?

King Nebuchadnezzar, king of Babylon, is one man who was in both of these places during his reign. Daniel 4 gives the account of his reign. Initially, the King was filled with pride. He reigned over a great and powerful nation, and he took full credit for it, giving no glory to God. He was deceived into thinking that his greatness was of his own doing. One day he was on the roof of his palace looking out over his kingdom and taking great pride in himself for his own glory.

> "Is not this great Babylon, which I have built by my mighty power as a royal residence and for the glory of my majesty?" Daniel 4:30 (ESV)

To make a long story short, God humbled him by removing him from his position and making him like a beast of the field. The king repented of his pride and took on a completely different view of himself and his kingdom. God restored him to power, but listen to his changed view.

At the end of the days I, Nebuchadnezzar, lifted my eyes to heaven, and my reason returned to me, and I blessed the Most High, and praised and honored him who lives forever, for his dominion is an everlasting dominion, and his kingdom endures from generation to generation; all the inhabitants of the earth are accounted as nothing, and he does according to his will among the host of heaven and among the inhabitants of the earth; and none can stay his hand or say to him, "What have you done?"

At the same time my reason returned to me, and for the glory of my kingdom, my majesty and splendor returned to me. My counselors and my lords sought me, and I was established in my kingdom, and still more greatness was added to me. **Now I, Nebuchadnezzar, praise and extol and honor the King of heaven, for all his works are right and his ways are just; and those who walk in pride he is able to humble.** Daniel 4:34-37 (ESV)

We are all faced with the same choices. We can live our lives seeking our own personal glory, or we can live them seeking the glory of God. It is a choice of our hearts. In most situations, we do not have to change what we are doing; we just need to have a change of heart that gives us a new perspective. Living apart from God—continually striving to establish our own recognition—is a hopeless endeavor that will never satisfy and can leave us in an empty and hopeless depression. In contrast, if we live our lives for the glory of God in all things, rather than the glory of man, we will experience the satisfaction, pleasure and blessings of God. We will have his rest for life, and experience his peace and joy in all we do. Which one do you want to pursue?

Seek First the Kingdom of God and Righteousness

Notice from the account of King Nebuchadnezzar that his kingdom was great before being humbled, but God blessed it with even more greatness after the king became humble and gave glory to God.

Jesus gives us a similar promise for seeking the glory of his kingdom first, rather than the glory of our own kingdoms.

"Therefore I tell you, do not be anxious about your life, what you will eat or what you will drink, nor about your body, what you will put on. Is not life more than food, and the body more than clothing? Look at the birds of the air: they neither sow nor reap nor gather into barns, and yet your heavenly Father feeds them. Are you not of more value than they? And which of you by being anxious can add a single hour to his span of life? And why are you anxious about clothing? Consider the lilies of the field, how they grow: they neither toil nor spin, yet I tell you, even Solomon in all his glory was not arrayed like one of these. But if God so clothes the grass of the field, which today is alive and tomorrow is thrown into the oven, will he not much more clothe you, O you of little faith? Therefore do not be anxious, saying, 'What shall we eat?' or 'What shall we drink?' or 'What shall we wear?' For the Gentiles seek after all these things, and your heavenly Father knows that you need them all. **But seek first the kingdom of God and his righteousness, and all these things will be added to you.** "Therefore do not be anxious about tomorrow, for tomorrow will be anxious for itself.

Sufficient for the day is its own trouble. Matthew 6:25-34 (ESV)

We are all seeking security. And we are all seeking purpose. Jesus is telling us that our security is found in our loving heavenly Father who watches over our lives and provides all things. He is also telling us that our first focus needs to be the establishment of his kingdom and his righteousness, not our kingdoms and our way of living. The pursuit of his kingdom and righteousness is our ultimate purpose in life. It is a purpose given to us by God, and it is a purpose for everyone. And he promises that if we put the purposes of his kingdom and righteousness first in our strivings that he will make sure we receive all of the earthly benefits as well.

78

Receiving earthly prosperity is of value for certain. But what good does it do if we receive all the things that the world chases after, if we still lack lasting purpose. *Lasting purpose satisfies. Wealth, position and power do not.* So how do we seek his kingdom and righteousness? What does that look like? And how do we achieve it?

First, we must understand that God created us for his purposes. We struggle in life because, in our rebellion, we want to live life for our own purposes. And that is how we get into trouble. Our own purposes do not lead to true life—God's do! So, if we want to pursue God's purposes, we are in agreement with God; he also wants us to pursue his purposes. He supports our desire. In fact, he was waiting for us to submit to his purposes and desires. He will accomplish his purposes in our lives; trust him.

The LORD will fulfill his purpose for me; your steadfast love, O LORD, endures forever. Do not forsake the work of your hands. Psalm 138:8 (ESV)

So call out to him. Pray that he will reveal his purposes for your life so that you can walk in them. He already knows your life and what he created you for. Just cry out to him for his purposes to manifest in your life.

I cry out to God Most High, to God who fulfills his purpose for me. Psalm 57:2 (ESV)

You may have your own ideas and aspirations for how God should use you. That is the wrong approach. It is not our plans that we should be asking God to anoint, bless and make happen. Instead, we should be seeking the Lord's purposes for our lives, and then obediently pursue them.

Many are the plans in a man's heart, but it is the LORD's purpose that prevails. Proverbs 19:21 (NIV)

And then it is imperative to understand that the grace of God is powerful. His grace is the power of God living within us to fulfill his purposes in us, through us and in this world for his good pleasure. We do not live out his purposes in our own strength. He will empower us. We just need to be seeking him and obediently walking in the steps he lays before us.

> ...for it is God who works in you to will and to act according to his good purpose. Philippians 2:13 (NIV)

God's kingdom is one of love, righteousness, truth, goodness, peace and joy. Who wouldn't want that? Does this sound like depression? Obviously not! Depression comes from living out our lives apart from God's kingdom purposes.

> For the Kingdom of God is not a matter of what we eat or drink, but of **living a life of goodness and peace and joy in the Holy Spirit**. If you serve Christ with this attitude, you will please God, and others will approve of you, too. Romans 14:17-18 (NLT)

So what does seeking his kingdom look like? Where do we start? It will be different for everyone, but there is a foundation for the establishment of his kingdom that is common to all of us. We must be filled with his Spirit and bear the fruit of his Spirit.

Once, when Jesus had just cast out a demon from a man, stated that his power to do so was by the Spirit of God. And he proclaimed that the coming of his Spirit was the evidence that the kingdom of God had come. (Matthew 12:28) Well, we have received the Spirit of God, and this Spirit lives within us and lives among us as the body of Christ. We have the power to live our lives by the power of the Holy Spirit of God who lives within us. This Spirit is the testimony of the kingdom of God.

Once, having been asked by the Pharisees when the kingdom of God would come, Jesus replied, "The kingdom of God does not come with your careful observation, nor will people say, 'Here it is,' or 'There it is,' because the **kingdom of God is within** [Or *among*]**you**." Luke 17:20-21 (NIV)

What should we be doing to seek the kingdom of God? First, we need to look like the kingdom of God; we need to be bearing the fruit of the Spirit.

But the fruit of the Spirit is love, joy, peace, patience, kindness, goodness, faithfulness, gentleness, self-control. Galatians 5:22-23 (ESV)

It does not matter what else we may do, if our nature is not being transformed into the character of God, then the kingdom of God is not being manifested in us. A kingdom has a king, and this King is Jesus Christ. But a kingdom also has the subjects of the King—people, and we are his people. Paul wrote that if we do not have love, we are nothing, gain nothing and we are just a bunch of noise. (1 Corinthians 13:1-3) We can do all sorts of things for God, but without love there will not be any power of the kingdom. We could be a prophet, a pastor, a miracle worker and even give up our lives, but without love it is all for nothing.

The pursuit to seek God's kingdom may be different for each one of us, but for every one of us it should look like God; it should bear the fruits of his Spirit. God is love. (1 John 4:8 & 16) If we are not walking in love, God will not be seen in us or among us.

Depression is the symptom of living without hope. We have the Spirit of God living within us so that we can become the subjects of God's kingdom by bearing the very character of God. This is our hope as Christians. There is no greater hope. There is no greater glory for us.

To them God chose to make known how great among the Gentiles are **the riches of the glory of this mystery,** which is **Christ in you, the hope of glory.** Colossians 1:27 (ESV)

That is the essence of his kingdom, and how this will be lived out is different for each one of us. We are all in different situations in life, but his kingdom can bear fruit in all of them. Think about it. How is his Spirit bearing fruit in you regarding your marriage? Does your family bear the fruit of the Spirit? When someone enters your home, what do they witness? This is a good place to start. No matter what else we may think we are doing for the Lord, if our own personal life is not bearing the fruit of the Spirit, it is not likely that we will be walking in the power of the Spirit in other places either. The kingdom of God is borne out in relationships. It is a kingdom of relationships. We need to assess our closest relationships and work there first. If we have a family, then our relationships with our spouse and our children need to be a first priority. This is seeking the kingdom of God and his righteousness first. The Scriptures are filled with instructions for marriage and family relationships. In fact, Jesus came to restore our relationship with God and with one another. Make that your central focus for following Christ.

In terms of our battle against depression, how joyful can we be if our family relationships are stressed, damaged, unforgiven, and lack harmony, love and unity? And in terms of seeking the things of the kingdom of God, how effective can we be in other places if our family is falling apart?

Seeking his kingdom comes in layers of priorities. As said, the first priority is our self—are we bearing the fruit of his Spirit, primarily love? The next layer or priority is the establishment of his kingdom in our closest relationships. In terms of priorities, God must be our first priority, and then marriage and family. If we fail at these, all other priorities lose their effectiveness and witness. In fact, how can we preach to others when we have failed to walk with Christ ourselves in our most fundamental relationships? (1 Timothy 3:4-5, 5:8, Titus 1:6) From there we can proceed to other relationships—neighbors, friends, work associates, members of the church—anyone we interact with.

The next layer or priority can be any place we work. This may be our employment at a company, business, organization or service. Are we working in these endeavors with the right motives, right heart, right thinking or understanding and with a kingdom purpose in all that we do? (Colossians 3:22-24, Ephesians 6:5-9)

This layer includes Christian ministries. All that we do is a Christian ministry. We are Christ's ambassadors wherever we work. (2 Corinthians 5:20) The world around us witnesses who we are by how we act, what we say, our attitudes, our viewpoints and whom we serve (Jesus). Relationships develop in all of our work. Do we reveal Jesus, or do we hide him. Jesus may make a place for us to disciple others directly through the teaching of his word. He may give us a specific designated place to promote his kingdom. We normally call this a ministry. But all of life is a ministry. And we must see the seeking of his kingdom and righteousness in all of life in all of its natural activities. Our character, our lives and our relationships should exude Jesus Christ, even without speaking about him, quoting scripture or exposing our Christian identity with outward apparel. There may be an opportunity to speak directly about God, but first we must be Christ to them—if he lives in you.

We were called by God to be a blessing to others. Being a blessing to others encompasses all that we do in all environments and situations. Our purpose as Christians is to be a blessing, to be a vessel for Jesus to bless others through us. The world is a place of selfish gain and retaliation. As Christians, we are the light of the world and the salt of the earth. (Matthew 5:13-16) We oppose the ways of the world by becoming a blessing that opposes every curse.

Don't repay evil for evil. Don't retaliate with insults when people insult you. Instead, pay them back with a blessing. That is what God has called you to do, and he will bless you for it. 1 Peter 3:9 (NLT)

To be Christ-like is to be a blessing, not expecting to have others bless you. Being a blessing is greater than being blessed. This is opposite to the way of the world. The world is one of "every man for himself". But the way of Christ is to bless others from our own resources and capabilities. What do we gain from it? We find the joy of being used to bless others. We experience the pleasure that it brings to Jesus and the affirmation of his love for us and his satisfaction in us. In this regard, "it is more blessed to give than to receive".

In all things I have shown you that by working hard in this way we must help the weak and remember the words of the Lord Jesus, how he himself said, **'It is more blessed to give than to receive.'"** Acts 20:35 (ESV)

We are to be hardworking contributors of society, doing something useful with our hands for the welfare of others. This is being Christ-like. This is acting like a citizen of the kingdom of God.

Let the thief no longer steal, but rather let him labor, doing honest work with his own hands, so that he may have something to share with anyone in need. Ephesians 4:28 (ESV)

Purpose drives productivity. Without purpose, we have empty lives. Empty lives are boring. We were created to be productive. Hobbies and recreation are fine, but they do not fill our need to be a functional member of society with a purpose within society. We were created for work from the beginning of creation.

We are not to be looking for how we can get more, but how we can serve more for the benefit of others. This is what it means to be a blessing. God created us to work for the welfare of all, and in this work we find joy and satisfaction. The idle struggle with depression out of boredom, a lack of purpose and because they have been cheated out of the blessings of work.

Consider all of this; it is our divine purpose! This is our calling from God! Live it out with all of your being! And depression will not overwhelm you because of a lack of purpose or worth in the eyes of God—or yourself.

Reflection Questions

Describe the meaning of your life? What are you doing that reflects this meaning?

Are you struggling with a lack of meaning and purpose in your life? How does that get you down?

In all of your strivings, has it still left you empty? How have your pursuits been self-serving, rather than for the welfare of others?

How have you been a servant who brings blessings to others? Start by describing how you serve and bless your family? How do you bless them in your relationships? How do you bless them as the spiritual leader of your home? Now describe how you bless those outside your home using these same criteria—relationships and leadership.

How do you use your life, your time, your talents and your sacrifice to be a productive contributor to the needs of mankind? What is your life-work? How do you work to supply the needs of others? How does that make you feel regarding joy over depression?

Chapter 7

Unforgiveness, Anger and Depression

Depression is the state of our hearts, but the needs of our hearts are not always so obvious. Our lives have several dimensions, some more obvious than others. We are all well aware of our physical existence. Our physical needs cannot go unnoticed. We all get hungry, which is a signal from our bodies that we need to eat. If we get cold, we put on more clothing and/or find a warmer place. If we are worn out, we find a place to rest. If we put our hand on a hot stove, it hurts and we quickly pull it back. We respond to the needs of our bodies naturally. It does not require any teaching or in-depth understanding.

Our minds are another dimension of our living being. We all have thoughts, but thoughts are not physical. We cannot touch a thought or weigh it on a scale. It has no mass, and it does not have dimensions. But we all experience our thoughts. Even though everyone's mind thinks automatically from birth, not all thoughts are good. In fact, much of our thinking can be harmful, and without warning. We can even believe a lie and allow the lie to lead us down a harmful path. Nearly all harmful addictive behaviors started out by believing a lie. We sought out the pleasure without seeing that we were planting the seeds of destroying our lives. Let me give a few examples.

Some say that a little gambling is just recreation. But after recreation comes another thought: gambling could make me rich. In the end gambling can take all we have. The phrase is, "steals me blind". In other words, it stole from me and I did not see it coming. Another example of how our minds lie to us: How could pornography hurt me? It's just the pleasure in my mind. How can it hurt my marriage if no one knows about my private behavior in my mind? But we don't see that in the end it will rob us of an intimate relationship with our spouse and eventually may destroy our marriage.

Our minds determine our behaviors, and our behaviors determine our outcomes. Having the right thoughts is critically important for a prosperous life. Look at Paul's instruction about renewing how we think.

> Don't copy the behavior and customs of this world, but let God transform you into a new person **by changing the way you think**. Then you will learn to know God's will for you, which is good and pleasing and perfect. Romans 12:2 (NLT)

Paul is saying that we have competition for our thoughts. The world around us tells one side, and God tells us another. The world lies to us, just like the addictions. God give us the truth, and it is opposed to the lies of the world. Now, which one will we choose? And if we choose God, will we pursue the truth he provides so that our minds will become renewed?

Remember, Adam and Eve were confronted with the same choice. God said that they would die if they ate of the tree of the knowledge of good and evil. But the devil came along and said, "You won't surely die." They had to choose who was lying to them, the devil or God. They decided that the devil was telling them the truth, and that God was the liar. We are in the same dilemma today. We can look to the world for what is true, or we can seek God. God gave us his written word, the Bible for the transformation of our thinking, but what have we chosen? Do we believe it is true? Do we read it? Do we make all kinds of excuses for not reading it?

Our minds are powerful, and they will determine the direction of our lives—for destruction or life.

Knowing our Heart

Our minds are very obvious to all of us. We all think, and we can consciously witness our thoughts, even if they are deceptive. But we have an even deeper part of our being that is not so obvious. Our heart is deep within us, and the understanding of our heart is hidden from most of us. For most of us, our heart drives our thinking and behavior, and we are unaware of the powerful activity of our own heart. The heart drives our lives, but we are mostly unaware of its activity. Look at what Jesus attributes to our hearts.

> For **out of the heart** come evil thoughts, murder, adultery, sexual immorality, theft, false witness, slander. Matthew 15:19 (ESV)

For most of us, our lives fall victim to our own heart. I say victim because an unredeemed heart can be like an unseen enemy of our life that lives deep within us and drives our thinking, attitudes, perspectives and behaviors.

When our feelings are hurt, it is our heart that incurs the pain. When we feel rejected, the feeling is from the heart. When something angers us, it is the heart that is angry. When we are frustrated or impatient, it is the heart that is reacting to the situation.

On the pleasant side, when we feel affirmed by someone's attention or words, it is our heart that feels good about ourselves. When we witness a beautiful sunset, a meadow of wild flowers, or any beauty of God's creation, it is our heart that feels elated. When we laugh, it is our heart that is responding to what we have seen or heard. Happiness and joy are of the heart.

We all have a need to love others and to be loved by others. This need comes from our heart. When we feel love for someone, it is our heart that is promoting the love and feeling the love of others. We all have a basic need to be connected with one another, and this connection is a flow of love. (Ephesians 4:16, Colossians 3:14)

Love is an act, which is driven by the heart, to give of ourselves for the welfare of others. When we are all living in love, we are beautifully connected to one another. *Depression cannot reside in such an atmosphere of loving unity.*

But just as love between us binds us together, offenses can divide us if we hold onto them in our heart. Selfishness is opposite to love. *As love looks out for the welfare of others, even at a cost to ourselves, our selfish side looks out for our personal welfare, even at the cost to others.* Love and selfishness are opposites. We all have a need to love and to be loved, but we are all born selfish. This is our sinful nature. We all have a sinful nature, so we all live in a world of offenses. The offenses have been occurring all of our lives. And the wounds and scars are ever present.

Where are these wounds and scars? They are in the heart. We may not be fully aware of what caused them, but the residual effects are there just the same. We are all walking around wounded or scarred to some degree. Feelings of insecurity, rejection, low esteem, failure, bitterness, and anger all reside in the heart. We sense the feelings, but we may be totally unaware of the root cause. It is like having undiagnosed cancer. It is eating us alive inside, but we don't know what is inside of us because we cannot see it. Only God fully sees and knows the state of our heart.

The heart is deceitful above all things, and desperately sick; who can understand it? "I the LORD search the heart and test the mind, to give every man according to his ways, according to the fruit of his deeds." Jeremiah 17:9-10 (ESV)

The NLT Bible says that the Lord "examines secret motives". Motives are even hidden or secret to ourselves. We need to be calling out to God to examine us like a physician to reveal what is truly going on inside.

Search me, O God, and **know my heart**; test me and know my anxious thoughts. See if there is any offensive way in me, and lead me in the way everlasting. Psalm 139:23-24 (NIV)

Depression is from the heart, and the root cause of our depression is not normally known. Only God can search it out and reveal the true ailment. We are all relational beings with a need to be loved and to love others. And since we are all sinners with a selfish sinful nature, it is common to be plagued with hurt, followed by unforgiveness, followed by bitterness—and followed by depression.

Unforgiveness, an Unresolved Debt

Remember, depression is founded on hopelessness. We all have a need to be loved and to love, but in this sinful world, we all experience offenses and give offenses. When offenses come upon us there are two typical responses. The first is to feel the pain of the offense. We feel the pain in our heart. It may be the pain of rejection, of being cheated, of being criticized, of having something stolen, of being abused, of a disloyal relationship, or any attack upon our personal welfare. The feeling of pain is our first response. The next response is most important. We can hold onto the offense or we can let it go—we can become bitter or we can forgive.

Sin may be defined as an offense against another person or God. Biblically, sin is described as a debt against someone. (Matthew 6:12, 18:21-35) Let's use the example of stealing. If I steal $100 from you, I have incurred a debt to you of $100. To forgive me is to cancel the debt. I would no longer owe you the $100. Now let's suppose that I stole, not $100, but $10,000 from you. That is a lot of money. It may have been easy to forgive my debt of $100, but you may be totally unwilling to forgive a debt of $10,000.

Now suppose that this offense happened a few years ago, and I have made no effort to repay you. If you have not forgiven the debt, how would you feel about me if you were in my presence? How would you feel about me every time you thought about me, or about how you are short $10,000. The pain of the offense can weigh heavy upon you for as long as the debt is still outstanding.

It is possible that I may come to you some day and repay the $10,000 that I stole from you. You would no longer have to forgive the monetary debt because I returned the money, but you would still have to forgive the fact that I intentionally took advantage of you. That is a debt also, and it could be the greatest one.

Most offenses cannot be repaid. For example, what if your spouse is unfaithful to you? There has been an adulterous affair. The unfaithfulness cannot be undone. It cannot be paid back. The debt incurred can be forgiven by you, but the debt cannot be returned. If you forgive the debt, your marriage can be restored. If you do not forgive the debt, the debt will always stand between you and your spouse. It will always eat away at your relationship. And it will always eat away at your own heart. A debt that is not soon forgiven turns into bitterness. And bitterness will likely turn into a counter offense. Now you have a debt incurred on both sides.

First you were hurt by your spouse's unfaithfulness. Now you are also hurt by your own bitterness. *Bitterness is a cancer of our own heart*. Unforgiveness, which leads to bitterness is self induced. It is like an offense to ourselves. *Bitterness is self-inflicted pain*. Bitterness can control and destroy our entire lives. It can drive us to medicate the pain of our hearts with addictions. It can shape our attitudes toward life, our attitude toward our self, our attitude toward others and God. It can rob us of happiness and joy. Even though the initial offense may have come from one specific person, we can become offensive to all those around us because we have held onto the offense and become bitter inside. We become a bitter person. Our lives feel the consequences on every side. What a hopeless existence. How depressing!!! Who will rescue me? The enemy lives within me; how can I be set free?

Rescued from the Enemy of Bitterness

Bitterness lives within the heart of man when he holds onto an unforgiven offense. So the resolution begins in the heart. First, we must understand that unforgiveness followed by bitterness is one of man's greatest enemies.

It lives within our hearts and lies to us by making us feel justified for having bitter thoughts and feelings toward another. It convinces us that we are the victim of someone else, and we are just acting in justifiable defense. Since we feel justified, we do not see that the real enemy is not the other person, but the bitterness itself that lives and grows within our own heart. Bitterness can rob us of life. It can deplete all joy. It has the power to destroy relationships far beyond the offender. It can consume our thinking, attitudes and behaviors. It can become the master of our feelings. It is a cancer of the soul. It fosters anxiety and hatred, and catalyzes depression. It is the enemy of our peace and joy, and all relationships. Who will rescue us from such a powerful foe that lives within the heart of man?

Jesus came to rescue us from just such captivity. John the Baptist's father, Zachariah, prophesied about the coming of Jesus. God spoke through him declaring that Jesus was sent to fulfill the oath to Abraham.

—to **rescue us from the hand of our enemies**, and to enable us to serve him without fear in holiness and righteousness before him all our days. Luke 1:74-75 (NIV)

We have many enemies. The devil and the world he rules over are our enemies. And the devil has many servants—men and women of this earth—who do his bidding, who are also our enemies. Death, the loss of life, is our enemy. We were not originally created to die. These enemies are serious and horrid, but there is one more enemy that is just as formidable—the sinful nature that is self focused and has the power to hold onto an offense, become bitter and consume our lives like a spiritual plague. Paul wrote about this enemy that lives within us. He describes our lack of power over this nature that drives us to destruction, and how powerless we are to overcome it. (Romans 7:14-25) He describes it as an inner war. And he asks the question, "Who will recue us?"

For I delight in the law of God in my inner being. But I see a different law in my members **waging war against the law of my mind and**

making me captive to the law of sin that is in my members. Wretched man that I am! **Who will rescue me from this body of death?** Thanks be to God through Jesus Christ our Lord! Romans 7:22-25 (NET)

Our sinful nature has power in many areas of life, unforgiveness and bitterness being only one, but a very destructive one. In our own strength, we are powerless to be set free of the resentment, unforgiveness and even hatred that grow deep roots within our own hearts. What hope do we have?

Jesus came to rescue us from this enemy. Jesus is our only hope for victory. We may struggle on our own in our own strength, but our power to overcome is insufficient. Jesus came, died for our forgiveness and reconciliation with God, and as a consequence, sent God's own Spirit to live within each one of us who have been chosen to be his own. It is by his Spirit within us that we now have his power to overcome.

Those who live according to the sinful nature have their minds set on what that nature desires; but those who live in accordance with the Spirit have their minds set on what the Spirit desires. The mind of sinful man is death, but the mind controlled by the Spirit is life and peace; the sinful mind is hostile to God. It does not submit to God's law, nor can it do so. Those controlled by the sinful nature cannot please God.

You, however, are controlled not by the sinful nature but by the Spirit, if the Spirit of God lives in you. And if anyone does not have the Spirit of Christ, he does not belong to Christ. But if Christ is in you, your body is dead because of sin, yet your spirit is alive because of righteousness. And if the Spirit of him who raised Jesus from the dead is living in you, he who raised Christ from the dead will also give life to your mortal bodies through his Spirit, who lives in you.

Therefore, brothers, we have an obligation—but it is not to the sinful nature, to live according to it. For if you live according to the sinful nature, you will die; but if **by the Spirit you put to death the misdeeds of the body, you will live**, Romans 8:5-13 (NIV)

Forgiveness: Power from God

Forgiveness is power. It is the power to destroy our spiritual enemies. Jesus defeated the devil by giving up his life for all of mankind who opposed him. Jesus carried the weight of every man's sin against God and man. He was rejected, mocked, lied about, tortured and hung on a cross to die. And as he hung on that cross, he cried out to God.

But Jesus said, "Father, forgive them, for they don't know what they are doing." Luke 23:34 (NET)

Jesus suffered at the hands of our sin, and he defeated the devil by forgiving us. He paid our debt against him. He had to make a choice to suffer at the hands of sinners in order to be victorious over sin. This sounds like foolishness in our human wisdom, but there is much greater power in forgiveness than retaliation.

When they hurled their insults at him, he did not retaliate; when he suffered, he made no threats. Instead, he entrusted himself to him who judges justly. He himself bore our sins in his body on the tree, so that we might die to sins and live for righteousness; by his wounds you have been healed. For you were like sheep going astray, but now you have returned to the Shepherd and Overseer of your souls. 1 Peter 2:23-25 (NIV)

Jesus did not have to suffer at the hands of men who despised him. He had the power to retaliate. He could have called upon his heavenly Father to rescue him, and all of mankind would have been wiped out. When the soldiers came to capture Jesus, Peter pulled out his sword and cut off the ear of one of them. But Jesus rebuked Peter, and he willingly gave himself up to his captors.

"Put your sword back in its place," Jesus said to him, "for all who draw the sword will die by the sword. Do you think I cannot call on my Father, and he will at once put at my disposal more than twelve legions of angels? Matthew 26:52-53 (NIV)

What is the point? We can have the same power to forgive. How can we win if we allow others to abuse and take advantage of us? Don't we deserve to hold onto the offense? They owe us! To forgive seems like foolishness. And from a worldly point of view, it is. That may be how the world views Jesus and his suffering.

For the message of the cross is foolishness to those who are perishing, but to us who are being saved it is the power of God. 1 Corinthians 1:18 (NIV)

Jesus was victorious over the devil by asking God to forgive those who hung him on his cross, and he asked while still hanging on it just prior to dying. Jesus instructs us to take up our cross daily, as he took up his.

Then he said to them all, "If anyone wants to become my follower, he must deny himself, take up his cross daily, and follow me. For whoever wants to save his life will lose it, but whoever loses his life for my sake will save it. For what does it benefit a person if he gains the whole world but loses or forfeits himself? Luke 9:23-25 (NET)

Jesus came to rescue us from our enemies, and one of our greatest enemies is holding onto unforgiveness. Bitterness and hatred toward someone else does more harm to us than it does to our offender. It eats us up inside. Jesus said that "whoever wants to save his life will lose it, but whoever loses his life for my sake will save it". This is from the previous verses where Jesus is referring to taking up our cross. This is a cross of forgiveness, and in Jesus' case, he forgave in the midst of the offense. There is victory in forgiveness.

We must all realize that our greatest enemy is not the one who has offended us; it is the unforgiveness that festers within us and robs us of our own life. It torments us and robs us of peace and joy. It can destroy our lives by destroying all other relationships. It leaves us hopelessly depressed. The real enemy lives within us. To be rescued is to be empowered to forgive, and then to walk in this power.

Forgiveness does not come naturally. Our nature—our sinful nature—is to hold onto the offense and to retaliate. But the nature of God is to have mercy and to forgive. Jesus commands us to forgive. Forgiveness is an act of obedience empowered by the Holy Spirit within us. In our own strength, under the rule of our sinful nature, we do not have the power to forgive. That is why Jesus gave us his own Spirit to live within us so that we would have his power to forgive. Forgiveness always means that we have to give up part of our life for our offender's. And *by giving up part of our life, we gain part of Jesus' life. That is a pretty good trade.*

Forgiveness is the only cure for bitterness and hatred. And when bitterness and hatred have eaten us up inside and sown the seeds of depression, forgiveness is our only deliverance. That is how Jesus rescues us. He doesn't just make the depression go away. He empowers us from within to release the debt incurred by our offender. We set them free, and we are also set free in the process. The alternative is bitterness, hatred and depression. *Forgiveness is the price paid to be set free.*

Unforgiveness is a very hopeless existence. Jesus came to give us hope, but this hope is only realized in our hearts when our hearts are transformed by his Spirit. We are called to love. The fruit of the Spirit is love. *Everyone has a created need to love. Forgiveness is an act of love. Forgiveness is the walk of a Christian.*

We are instructed to guard our hearts.

Guard your heart above all else, for it is the source of life. Proverbs 4:23 (HCSB)

It would be easy to deceive ourselves, thinking that guarding my heart is to protect myself from the offenses of others. In other words, I need to be tough. I need to have the upper hand of strength against my foe. From a worldly view, being the stronger one may seem necessary to protect ourselves. Being the stronger one may protect our body or situation, but it does not protect our heart. Jesus told us to love our enemies, to turn the other cheek when struck, to give more when something is taken from us and to serve more when being forced to serve. We are not to resist an evil person. (Matthew 5:38-48) In doing these things, we are the ones who are victorious. We are the ones affirmed by God. This seems so contrary to our view of survival, but true survival is freedom from bitterness, hatred and depression. True survival is in the heart of man. Forgiveness is the key to having much more than survival—to have victory in this life (and for the next). Forgiveness unites us with others. Unity and peace is victory.

> Bear with each other and forgive whatever grievances you may have against one another. Forgive as the Lord forgave you. And over all these virtues put on love, which binds them all together in perfect unity. Colossians 3:13-14 (NIV)

To "bear with each other" is to accept one another, to invite others into your life without protective barriers, to make allowances for their faults. To forgive is to cancel the debt of offenses, even as they happen. *People who are easily offended are overly self-focused, and they will never fully enjoy other people. Their judgments will rob themselves of joy. Their rejection of others will rob themselves of intimate unity with others, which we all need. It will leave them hopelessly alone in life. With hopelessness comes depression. It may appear that others don't like you, but it is more a matter that you may not like others.*

You may find that you are easily irritated or angered by others. Realize that irritation or anger toward others is a sign of an unforgiving attitude. It is a sign that you have taken offense and that you are harboring the offense in your heart. The anger lives within you like a parasite, and it is eating away at your joy, ruining your relationships and planting the seeds of bitterness and depression. The anger in itself may not be sin, but we can allow the anger to drive us to sin. We are instructed to guard our hearts. When we witness anger brewing within us, we need to be silent and find out what is going on inside, and then deal with it. Forgiveness is likely the remedy.

In your anger **do not sin**; when you are on your beds, **search your hearts and be silent**. Psalm 4:4 (NIV)

We cannot walk in love and also walk around being easily offended by others. They are opposites. It is our choice to love, which means that it is our choice to forgive and to be joyful and to appreciate others. Love is good medicine for all of us. On the other hand, irritability and holding onto the wrongs of others against us will make our hearts sick.

Love is patient and kind. Love is not jealous or boastful or proud or rude. It does not demand its own way. **It is not irritable**, and it **keeps no record of being wronged**. It does not rejoice about injustice but rejoices whenever the truth wins out. Love never gives up, never loses faith, is always hopeful, and endures through every circumstance. 1 Corinthians 13:4-7 (NLT)

The key to all this is to be others-focused rather than self-focused. It is to be more concerned and interested in others than for others to be more concerned and interested in us. The offenses of others may not even be felt when we have taken the focus of our hearts off of ourselves and placed it on others.

My dear brothers, take note of this: Everyone should be quick to listen, slow to speak and **slow to become angry**, for **man's anger does not bring about the righteous life that God desires**. James 1:19-20 (NIV)

Being "quick to listen" and "slow to speak" is a matter of being others-focused. When we are more caring about others, we will not be so vulnerable to becoming offended, irritated and angry ourselves. This is how we are to walk righteously before God. Walking in loving acceptance and forgiveness is righteousness.

Jesus was quite clear about having mercy toward others and forgiving them from our heart. He taught us to pray, "forgive us our debts as we have forgiven our debtors". In other words, we are asking God to forgive us as we forgive others. The measure we use will be the measure he uses for us.

> Do not judge, so that you won't be judged. For with the judgment you use, you will be judged, and with the measure you use, it will be measured to you. Matthew 7:1-2 (HCSB)

Jesus followed the "Lord's Prayer" explaining that if we do not forgive other, that our heavenly Father would not forgive us.

> For if you forgive others their sins, your heavenly Father will also forgive you. But if you do not forgive others, your Father will not forgive you your sins. Matthew 6:14-15 (NET)

We may say that it is too hard to forgive the offenses of others. We have been victimized, and they owe us. How can we be the ones at fault? But God looks at all of us and sees right into our hearts. He knows that we have all sinned and fall short of his glory. (Romans 3:23) We are all in need of his forgiveness. Jesus died for all mankind, every one of us. But his forgiveness is not imparted if we do not show mercy and forgiveness to others. This should be all the motivation we need to forgive the debts of others against us. Jesus could not have been clearer about this. (Matthew 18:21-35)

When we forgive, we are cancelling someone else's debt against us. But a closer look at forgiveness reveals that we are the ones set free. The offending person may have his debt canceled, but we are being set free from bitterness, which leads to depression and a rotting away of our souls. The one who forgives has the greater gain. Our deliverance should be motivation enough to forgive. But this deliverance is only temporary, lasting only for as long as we may live. Being forgiven for our sins by God is eternal, and will determine the state of our eternal existence. It should be very clear that forgiving the debts of others against us is really a small price to pay for what we will receive now in this life and the life after for eternity.

Forgiving Ourselves

So far we have discussed our forgiveness of others, but we have not mentioned forgiving ourselves. God's word clearly tells us that he forgives us through Jesus Christ. But all too often, we do not forgive ourselves. And when we find ourselves in bondage to our own unforgiveness, we may even lose the comfort of knowing that God loves us and forgives us.

Regretful Guilt

Some past sins do not have a significant effect on our lives today, so those may not be the ones that we hold onto in unforgiveness. For example, maybe you used to lie and manipulate others for your own selfish gain, but today you are not like that, and your relationships with others are based on serving and caring for others. Chances are that you are not dragged down by these past sins—you have forgiven yourself as God has forgiven you through Christ Jesus.

But now let's suppose that you were a drug addict in years past, and because of your addiction your marriage and your relationships with your children were ruined. Your wife divorced you and you are presently estranged from your children. The regret of your past behavior haunts you. You have incurred a heavy price for your past sin, and even though you are no longer taking drugs, the damage has already taken its toll and you see no hope for restoring what was lost. You hold yourself in regretful unforgiveness.

Regret is very painful, but our hope is still in the future that God has for us. Only God can redeem our past. He may not go back and undo the damage we did (although that too can happen), but he still has a glorious future for all of us who live in him. Remember, when we come to Christ, our lives belong to Christ. Or just as important, the life we live, we live in Christ. We have a new life, and it is a new live in Christ, for Christ and with an eternal destiny. Our old life did not have this hope. We have a new hope now—an eternal hope because we belong to Christ.

> I have been crucified with Christ, and it is no longer I who live, but Christ lives in me. So the life I now live in the body, I live because of the faithfulness of the Son of God, who loved me and gave himself for me. Galatians 2:20 (NET)

We cannot go back and undo the past, but we can go forward, striving for the high calling of God for an eternal future that is filled with true life.

Paul lived an awful life before Christ Jesus came to him. He was crucifying Christians. He had them put in prison and many he had stoned to death. How might he have felt about his past? But look at his own words about himself and his future focus.

> Not that I have already attained this—that is, I have not already been perfected—but I strive to lay hold of that for which Christ Jesus also laid hold of me. Brothers and sisters, I do not consider myself to have attained this. Instead I am single-minded: **Forgetting the things that are behind and reaching out for the things that are ahead**, with this goal in mind, **I strive toward the prize of the upward call of God in Christ Jesus.** Philippians 3:12-14 (NET)

We have a new life in Jesus Christ. That should be the focus for every Christian—no regret with a hopeful focus. We forgive our past mistakes because we have a glorious future ahead of us through Christ. The life we are striving for is infinitely more than the one we left behind, no matter what we may have lost.

False Guilt

Many of us were raised in very judgmental environments. We may have had a very critical and angry father or mother who was perpetually disappointed in us. He/she may have rarely, if ever, affirmed us, but continually expressed disgust. You may have done everything possible to get your parent's approval and affirmation, but with no avail. You never measured up to their standard. Now you are older, but you still live in the belief that you lack worth and are forever guilty for something, even if that "something" is not obvious. You find yourself apologizing for every insignificant and unintended infraction. For example, if you choose a chair to sit in, but then think that someone else may have wanted that chair, you apologize and offer to get up so they can sit there. You are forever giving in to someone else's will at the expense of your own. You act as though your opinions are automatically inferior to the opinions of others, and you find yourself apologizing for them and giving in to the will of others. False guilt rules your life, and you do not feel good about yourself. It becomes a self-imposed trap, and you cannot forgive yourself because you do not have a righteous opinion of yourself.

We may not have had a father or mother who loved us, nurtured us, encouraged us and affirmed us. But now we do! Our heavenly Father knows our shortcomings, but they do not count anymore. What counts is what we are becoming because he loves us and has provided everything we need to obtain his divine nature.

By his divine power, God has given us everything we need for living a godly life. We have received all of this by coming to know him, the one who called us to himself by means of his marvelous glory and excellence. And because of his glory and excellence, he has given us great and precious promises. These are the promises that enable you to share his divine nature and escape the world's corruption caused by human desires. 2 Peter 1:3-4 (NLT)

There are many verses in this regard—too many to reference here. Read your Bible, and believe what you read. Then obediently walk in the way Jesus directs you. And you will no longer walk in false guilt. You will not have to forgive yourself, because false guilt is not based on sin, but false accusations.

We have a new Father now—God Almighty. And he loves us enough to forgive all of our sins, and to fill us by his very own Spirit so that we can have his life, his character and his power living within us. This is our true identity and our eternal hope.

How great is the love the Father has lavished on us, that we should be called children of God! And that is what we are! The reason the world does not know us is that it did not know him. Dear friends, now we are children of God, and what we will be has not yet been made known. But we know that **when he appears, we shall be like him**, for we shall see him as he is. **Everyone who has this hope in him purifies himself, just as he is pure**. 1 John 3:1-3 (NIV)

Guilt Over Unrepentant Sin

Our call to follow Christ begins with a call to repent of our sins. This means that we are to change the direction of our lives from one of willful sin to one of willfully following Christ by the empowerment and leading of his Spirit within us and as instructed by the word of God. If you are feeling guilty and cannot forgive yourself, it may be because you are still acting in sin, knowing that you are willfully doing what is wrong in the eyes of God and of yourself. Why can't you forgive yourself? Because you are not forgiven by God. You are guilty! So repent and be forgiven.

And so John came, baptizing in the desert region and preaching a baptism of **repentance for the forgiveness of sins**. Mark 1:4 (NIV)

Peter said to them, "**Repent**, and each one of you be baptized in the name of Jesus Christ **for the forgiveness of your sins**, and you will receive the gift of the Holy Spirit. Acts 2:38 (NET)

Therefore **repent and turn back so that your sins may be wiped out, so that times of refreshing may come** from the presence of the Lord, and so that he may send the Messiah appointed for you—that is, Jesus. Acts 3:19-20 (NET)

Repentance is great and effective medication for guilt and depression. Drugs and alcohol and other addictions are medication too, but they do not cure; they only cover up the guilt for a while until you get sober. Then the guilt multiplies. Repentance followed by forgiveness is the only true reliever.

Reflection Questions

Are you typically bitter or angry inside? What wounds inside are you feeling?

Think of the significant people in your life from your childhood until now. Which of those relationships are damaged or broken? How do those severed relationships or the memory of them affect you today?

Who do you hold in unforgiveness? How difficult would it be to forgive them? How difficult would it be to reconcile those relationships?

How much of your depression is due to your unforgiveness of those who offended you?

Have you forgiven yourself? Why are you still in bondage to unforgiveness of yourself? What must you do to be free?

Chapter 8

Low Self-Worth

This life is one huge battle between light and darkness, between what is true and what is not true (a lie). Think about the temptation presented by the devil to Adam and Eve. God clearly told them not to eat of the tree of the knowledge of good and evil because if they did, they would die. But then the serpent, the devil, came along and essentially called God a liar. He denied that God was telling them the truth, and that he was lying to them to prevent them from having the power of God's knowledge.

"You will not surely die," the serpent said to the woman. "For God knows that when you eat of it your eyes will be opened, and you will be like God, knowing good and evil." Genesis 3:4-5 (NIV)

Jesus called the devil the birthplace of all lies. The devil lied through the serpent to Adam and Eve. He lies to us through our culture, through media propaganda, the government and he lies to us through other people. For example, today we are being told that homosexuality is a normal trait that some people have, and that they were born with it. We are told to accept such behavior as normal, and anyone who opposes this view is hateful. For whatever reason, our movies and TV programs are flooded with homosexuals with a highly disproportionate representation of homosexuality. We are being brainwashed by media to accept this new norm as wholesome and normal. The US government has decreed homosexuality as a born trait that is no different than being born a certain race or sex, male or female. It is now a crime to discriminate against homosexuality as an unhealthy or morally wrong behavior. Many corporations have adopted policies so that homosexuals are fully accepted in the workforce. As Bible believing Christians, the word of God clearly speaks contrary to these views. But like the serpent with Adam and Eve, we are being told that God is the liar, and that our culture has the real truth on this matter.

Lies are all about us. Lies will lead us down destructive paths in life. We have the devil promoting lies to lead us astray, and we have God, who is the embodiment of truth, to lead us down the path of life. Jesus called the Pharisees the children of the devil because they denied what was true and promoted lies.

> You people are from your father the devil, and you want to do what your father desires. He was a murderer from the beginning, and does not uphold the truth, because there is no truth in him. Whenever he lies, he speaks according to his own nature, because **he is a liar and the father of lies**. John 8:44 (NET)

Jesus and the devil are diametrically opposed based on truth. The devil is the source of lies, and Jesus is the embodiment of all truth. Lies lead to death, and truth leads to life.

> Jesus said to him, "I am the way, and the truth, and the life. No one comes to the Father except through me. John 14:6 (ESV)

How does the devil take us captive? It is mainly through lies. He manipulates our thinking such that we follow his ways. He manipulates our thinking to cripple us. We have already revealed how the devil lies to us through outside sources, such as the media, culture, the government, other people and the like. As with the Pharisees in Jesus' time, the devil was lying through the heads of the "church". They are the ones who incited the government and the people to crucify Jesus.

These are lying sources that exist outside of our own being, but what if the devil can lie to us from inside our own mind. How might he do that?

To explain how that can happen, let's first lay one more foundation: Love and truth are harmoniously connected as one. And lies and evil are also harmoniously connected. In other words, if a child is raised in an environment of love, he will likely believe that he has value in God's sight and others (truth). In contrast, if he was raised in an unloving environment, he will likely struggle with his worth in the eyes of God or others (a lie).

Let's look at a few verses on these opposing pairs: Love and truth, and Evil and lies.

Love and Truth

Love does not delight in evil but rejoices with the **truth**. 1 Corinthians 13:6 (NIV)

Instead, speaking the **truth** in **love**, we will in all things grow up into him who is the Head, that is, Christ. Ephesians 4:15 (NIV)

You have purified your souls by obeying the **truth** in order to show sincere mutual **love**. So **love** one another earnestly from a pure heart. 1 Peter 1:22 (NET)

Evil and Lies

You love **evil** more than good, **lies** more than speaking the truth. Psalm 52:3 (NET)

The coming of the lawless one will be in accordance with the work of Satan displayed in all kinds of counterfeit miracles, signs and wonders, and in every sort of **evil** that **deceives** those who are perishing. They perish because they refused to love the **truth** and so be saved. For this reason God sends them a powerful delusion so that they will **believe**

the lie and so that all will be condemned who have not believed the **truth** but have **delighted in wickedness**. 2 Thessalonians 2:9-12 (NIV)

His mouth is full of curses and **lies** and threats; **trouble and evil** are under his tongue. Psalm 10:7 (NIV)

The scoundrel's weapons are destructive; he hatches plots to destroy the needy with **lies**, even when the poor says what is right. Isaiah 32:7 (HCSB)

No one is concerned about justice; no one sets forth his case truthfully. They depend on **false words and tell lies**; they conceive of oppression and **give birth to sin**. Isaiah 59:4 (NET)

So how does love bare the truth? And how does evil bare the lies? Let's start with love and truth. Suppose a child is raised in a family of very loving parents. His father and mother have a very good marriage. Their loving commitment to each other is clearly seen within his home. And let's suppose that they sincerely love their child. They encourage him, value him, cherish him, protect him, provide for him, nurture him, spend time with him, train and teach him, and discipline him for his own good without anger or disgust. They would also speak truthful words to him and they would tell him how valuable he was to them. These words are important, but even without such words, he would know he was sincerely loved because his parents lives speak of love for him.

How do you think this child would view himself as a consequence of being loved? Most likely he would see himself as having value in the sight of others. He would see himself as having value, even in the face of personal failure. He would be confident and secure. This view of himself was promoted by the love he experienced from his dad and mom. His source of truth came from the love that was shown by his parents.

Now let's consider a different child that was raised in an unloving home—an evil home. His parents did not love each other. They frequently had fights and yelled at each other using degrading words. There was always tension and anger. Divorce was always on the forefront, and eventually occurred. After the divorce the boy's dad and mom lived in two different houses, and he spent time with them separately in each of their houses. This child's life is not secure. There is no nurturing or encouragement. In fact, he is usually being yelled at and degraded. His parents are normally angry and disgusted with him. He is not disciplined, and in fact, each parent spoils him in order to win favor over the other parent. Even though he is spoiled, he does not feel valued. In fact, he feels manipulated and controlled. He also experiences physical and sexual abuse. Even though there are people around him, he feels all alone in this world.

How do you think this child views himself? Worthless? A failure? Unlovable? Hopeless?

Both children have a view of themselves based upon how they were treated by their parents. Which one has a truthful view of himself? If your dad frequently discouraged you does that mean you are useless? If your dad frequently encouraged you, does that mean you are a success? Chances are that if you were discouraged, you see yourself as a useless failure with a hopeless future. And if you were regularly built up, you probably see yourself as a valuable asset to society with a good future. Who do you think will struggle with depression?

Hopefully, you get the point. Our view of ourselves is highly influenced by the view projected upon us by our parent's behavior. We struggle to change this view. And it becomes a struggle because we tend to strongly believe that this view is true. Furthermore, when we have a low opinion of ourselves, we usually live up to that opinion—positive or negative. It is very difficult to excel in life when we view ourselves as worthless and unlovable.

We may not have grown up in a terrible home, but we may have been born with some characteristics that made us feel inferior to our peers. We have hundreds of labels today. ADHD is a big one today. I hear so many kids and adults comment about themselves, "I have ADHD". And their use of the label indirectly says, "I am a handicapped cripple. I can't help myself. I have an excuse." In essence, we believe lies about ourselves based on how we are treated by others and what labels have been put on us.

What we think about ourselves has the greatest power to rob us of life or to excel in life. Most of us believe degrading lies about ourselves that rob us of life. Knowing that we come up short, and believing that it is all because we lack value and capability is the real handicap. This hopeless belief and attitude about our self and life is the breeding ground for depression. So what can we do about it? How can we transform our thinking? If we already believe that we are hopeless victims of our own shortcomings, what hope is there?

Knowing the Truth about Our Self

What is the lie that we believe about our self? "If we have loving parents, we have value." "If we have unloving parents, we lack value."

What is the truth? First, we live in a world of fallen sinners—every one of us. From this regard, we are all the same. The only true worth that anyone has comes from God. If we aspire to him, we can have great worth. If we do not, anything that we may think we have is of no value. That includes money, skills, status, position, good looks, power, charisma, popularity, material possession and anything else this world values— they're all worthless without an intimate relationship with God.

Jesus died for our sins so that we can become children of God. God loves his children. With God, all things are possible. With God, it is not what we are that is so important, but what we are becoming through God. As children of God, we become the righteousness of God. Our only worth comes from belonging to God as one of his children.

God the Father sent his Son for two reasons. First, Jesus was sent to die for the forgiveness of our sins so that our relationship with God could be reconciled. And, two, now that we are reconciled, we can become children of God by being born again of his Spirit. In other words, God gives us a new nature that literally lives within us by God's indwelling Holy Spirit. For those of us who have become God's children, that is who we are now and forever. That is our true and lasting identity. Christ lives within us. The eternal God has given us his eternal life through a new birth into his kingdom and family.

> Blessed be the God and Father of our Lord Jesus Christ! By his great mercy he gave us **new birth into a living hope** through the resurrection of Jesus Christ from the dead, that is, into an inheritance imperishable, undefiled, and unfading. It is reserved in heaven for you, who by God's power are protected through faith for a salvation ready to be revealed in the last time. 1 Peter 1:3-5 (NET)

> To them God has chosen to make known among the Gentiles the glorious riches of this mystery, which is **Christ in you, the hope of glory**. Colossians 1:27 (NIV)

We have a "living hope", which is "Christ in you, the hope of glory". The God who created the entire universe–the one who created mankind, this awesome, loving, living God–has given us his own Spirit to live within us who believe and are called according to his purposes. No matter what family background we came from, we now have become members of God's family when we believed and received his forgiveness and his Spirit for the power of a new life. We are his now, and we have a glorious future that is kept safe in heaven for us. We are part of God's purposes, and we live for those purposes here and now.

> And we know that all things work together for good for those who love God, who are **called according to his purpose**, because those whom he foreknew he also predestined to be conformed to the image of his Son, that his Son would be the firstborn among many brothers and sisters. And those he predestined, he also **called**; and those he called, he also **justified**; and those he justified, he also **glorified**. Romans 8:28-30 (NET)

No matter what our past, we do not live in the past. We are a new creation with a new power living within us and a new future to live for and hope in.

> So then, if anyone is in Christ, he is a new creation; what is old has passed away—look, what is new has come! 2 Corinthians 5:17 (NET)

We can look back and see all of the abuse upon us. We can see all of the sin that we selfishly lived out at the expense of others. We can see our wrongdoing, shortcomings and guilt. But all that is washed away by the blood of Jesus. Through Jesus we have the hope of becoming the righteousness of God.

> God made the one who did not know sin to be sin for us, so that in him we would become the righteousness of God. 2 Corinthians 5:21 (NET)

We have a glorious hope. It is a hope of becoming like Jesus Christ in all of his perfection, in all of his glory and in all of his character. We have been given his Spirit so that we can begin to bear the fruit of his Spirit now in this life and to enjoy the benefits of becoming like Jesus. (Galatians 5:22-23) We are on a journey, and the path leads to perfection, and perfection leads to eternal life. (Matthew 7:13-14, Romans 6:22-23) We have not reached all of his perfection yet, but we know that when we see him face-to-face, we will be instantly perfected by being transformed into his likeness. And, the old sinful nature that continually tugs at us will be completely destroyed. (1 Corinthians 15:42-54) All that will be left is the powerful nature of God's Spirit that lives within and among us who believe and who now belong to God as his children. There is great joy for those who are being transformed into the likeness of Jesus, and have the promise of its completion when we see Jesus face-to-face.

> See what kind of love the Father has given to us, that we should be called children of God; and so we are. The reason why the world does

not know us is that it did not know him. Beloved, we are God's children now, and what we will be has not yet appeared; but we know that when he appears we shall be like him, because we shall see him as he is. And everyone who thus hopes in him purifies himself as he is pure. 1 John 3:1-3 (ESV)

In this life, as Christians, we are on the hard and narrow road that leads to perfection. (Matthew 7:13-14) Not everyone is traveling this road that leads to eternal life. We who are on the road to life should have great joy, for we are being perfected into the image of life—Jesus Christ. We have the life of God living within us. What hope! What joy! We have a purpose and a divine destiny.

And this is the testimony: God has given us eternal life, and this life is in his Son. **He who has the Son has life; he who does not have the Son of God does not have life.** I write these things to you who believe in the name of the Son of God so that you may know that you have eternal life. 1 John 5:11-13 (NIV)

We can look around and compare ourselves to others. Some have money. Some have successful careers. Some are looked up to for their accomplishments. Some are popular and seem to have many friends. Some do not appear to struggle with life (which is mostly a lie). But there is one thing that awaits us all—death. This life is actually quite short. And the older we get, the years seem to pass by more quickly. My wife and I like to visit cemeteries. We live in a town with graves of some famous people. But their lives are like everyone else. As Solomon once wrote, we all share in a common destiny—death. (Ecclesiastes 9:2-3) We all have a beginning and an ending point. In the end, the real concern is not how long we lived or how prosperous we were in this world. The real concern is who we lived for while in this life on earth. Asapth, the psalmist, gives a lament as a man looks at the rich and successful people, and as depression wells up in him over his own decrepit life. Then God reveals to him their final destiny—

death and destruction. (Psalm 73) *Our joy comes from keeping an eternal focus.* This life is short; eternity is forever. Hope comes from focusing on our eternal destiny, not today's prosperity. What is our hope? "In Christ we are made alive." The enemy of death will be defeated, and we will have true life, eternal life. There is no depression in true life. Only Christians have this joyful hope.

> For as in Adam all die, so also in Christ shall all be made alive. But each in his own order: Christ the firstfruits, then at his coming those who belong to Christ. Then comes the end, when he delivers the kingdom to God the Father after destroying every rule and every authority and power. For he must reign until he has put all his enemies under his feet. The last enemy to be destroyed is death. 1 Corinthians 15:22-26 (ESV)

> But let me reveal to you a wonderful secret. We will not all die, but we will all be transformed! It will happen in a moment, in the blink of an eye, when the last trumpet is blown. For when the trumpet sounds, those who have died will be raised to live forever. And we who are living will also be transformed. For our dying bodies must be transformed into bodies that will never die; our mortal bodies must be transformed into immortal bodies. 1 Corinthians 15:51-53 (NLT)

Death is our enemy. The devil is our enemy, and the world he rules over. The devil is a thief. He comes to devour us, to rob us of life. Our hope is not in the devil's world; our hope is in the kingdom of God. That is where we find true life. Jesus came to give us his kingdom, to make us citizens of his kingdom.

> The thief comes only to steal and kill and destroy. I came that they may have life and have it abundantly. John 10:10 (ESV)

Listen, my dear brothers: Has not God chosen those who are poor in the eyes of the world to be rich in faith and to inherit the kingdom he promised those who love him? James 2:5 (NIV)

Depression comes from having a hopeless, despairing view of our lives. Well, this life is hopeless and despairing; that's reality. But we have a hope that is beyond this life, and not everyone has this hope. We live in a fallen world, but nothing in this world can rob us of this hope. Our hope is in God, kept in heaven for us.

Blessed be the God and Father of our Lord Jesus Christ! According to his great mercy, he has caused us to be born again to a living hope through the resurrection of Jesus Christ from the dead, to an inheritance that is imperishable, undefiled, and unfading, kept in heaven for you, who by God's power are being guarded through faith for a salvation ready to be revealed in the last time. In this you rejoice, though now for a little while, if necessary, you have been grieved by various trials, so that the tested genuineness of your faith—more precious than gold that perishes though it is tested by fire—may be found to result in praise and glory and honor at the revelation of Jesus Christ. Though you have not seen him, you love him. Though you do not now see him, you believe in him and rejoice with joy that is inexpressible and filled with glory, obtaining the outcome of your faith, the salvation of your souls. 1 Peter 1:3-9 (ESV)

We have been given a deposit of the Holy Spirit of God to live within us as a guarantee of our glorious future which will be revealed when we return to Jesus in eternity. (2 Corinthians 1:22, 5:5, 2 Timothy 1:14) And as we live out our years on this earth, we are loved by God as his possession. We live in a dark world, but we live for his purposes to bring forth his light and glory. Nothing can take that from us.

And we know that for those who love God all things work together for good, for those who are called according to his purpose. For those whom he foreknew he also predestined to be conformed to the image of his Son, in order that he might be the firstborn among many brothers. And those whom he predestined he also called, and those whom he called he also justified, and those whom he justified he also glorified.

What then shall we say to these things? If God is for us, who can be against us? He who did not spare his own Son but gave him up for us all, how will he not also with him graciously give us all things? Who shall bring any charge against God's elect? It is God who justifies. Who is to condemn? Christ Jesus is the one who died—more than that, who was raised—who is at the right hand of God, who indeed is interceding for us. Who shall separate us from the love of Christ? Shall tribulation, or distress, or persecution, or famine, or nakedness, or danger, or sword? As it is written,

> "For your sake we are being killed all the day long; we are regarded as sheep to be slaughtered."

No, in all these things we are more than conquerors through him who loved us. For I am sure that neither death nor life, nor angels nor rulers, nor things present nor things to come, nor powers, nor height nor depth, nor anything else in all creation, will be able to separate us from the love of God in Christ Jesus our Lord. Romans 8:28-39 (ESV)

This is the truth. There are many Scripture references given in this section. They are given so that you can cling to them as the absolute truth. Any negative thinking that has bound you in the past is a lie, for you now belong to Christ. Your future is hidden in him.

Since, then, you have been raised with Christ, set your hearts on things above, where Christ is seated at the right hand of God. **Set your minds on things above, not on earthly things**. For you died, and your life is now hidden with Christ in God. When Christ, who is your life, appears, then you also will appear with him in glory. Colossians 3:1-4 (NIV)

This is the truth, and the truth will set you free. Jesus came to set you free; live in his freedom. There is no cause to be depressed any longer. You have a new life in Christ Jesus.

Then Jesus said to those Judeans who had believed him, "If you continue to follow my teaching, you are really my disciples and you will know the truth, and **the truth will set you free**." John 8:31-32 (NET)

Identity

Who am I? We were created with an identity need. I belong to someone. Typically, a child takes his or her father's last name. And when a woman marries, she typically takes on her husband's last name. And then, their children take the same last name. We belong to our family. That is our identity.

But what happens when our family abuses us? What about the identity? On the one hand, we were born into a family, and our identity is there, and under our father. That is how God ordained it. But what if my family is dysfunctional, abusive, harmful, rejecting, angry and filled with division and conflict? I have a need to identify, but my need is confronted with rejection and worthlessness from the very ones whom I look to for encouragement, closeness and support. What a hopeless and depressing dilemma.

Many who find themselves in this situation spend their lives trying to obtain encouragement, closeness and support from the ones who continually discourage, are distant and are not uplifting. Resentment and bitterness grow because your identity with your family is not fulfilling, but painful. It becomes a continuous struggle, always trying to fulfill your heartfelt need from the ones that God had appointed to love you. So now you struggle on your own to have an identity. Many find that identity elsewhere. Many seek their peers, but that can give rise to just another struggle. Some seek marriage, hoping to find their identity in their spouse. But when identity with their father and mother has never been fulfilled, marriage typically fails them too. And then divorce may come, which leaves them alone and battling the same struggle all over again and again.

The question continues to haunt us, "Who am I?" We were created with the need to identify with other living beings. This is a fundamental need that we all have that was given to us by God. When we struggle to find identity, we struggle with ourselves. And when we continually come up short, we struggle with depression.

The struggle begins early in life, because the struggle begins with our earthly family. Teenagers seek identity outside of their family to make up for the lack of wholesome identity at home. Now they have to struggle in two arenas, their family and their peers. Far too many end up medicating their hopeless struggle with drugs, alcohol, becoming a cutter, and other destructive behaviors. And many attempt suicide, and many succeed.

The lack of identity and the fruitless struggle to obtain it becomes our own enemy that has the power to rob us of life, contentment and joy. Jesus came to rescue us from our enemies. (Luke 1:67-79) He has become our identity. The identity of our earthly family is temporary because our lives are temporary. But our heavenly family is eternal. Our heavenly Father is eternal. The body of Christ is eternal. Our eternal identity is hidden in Christ. Our need to belong has been fulfilled. We have been purchased by God through Jesus, and we now belong to him through Christ. We have been given his Spirit that lives within us and proclaims his ownership of us and our identity with him. We are now his family members and live as part of his household.

If then you have been raised with Christ, seek the things that are above, where Christ is, seated at the right hand of God. Set your minds on things that are above, not on things that are on earth. For you have died, and **your life is hidden with Christ in God**. When **Christ who is**

your life appears, then you also will appear with him in glory. Colossians 3:1-4 (ESV)

You also are among them, called to **belong to Jesus Christ**. Romans 1:6 (NET)

For this reason I kneel before the Father, from whom **his whole family in heaven and on earth derives its name**. Ephesians 3:14-15 (NIV)

Do you not know that your body is a temple of **the Holy Spirit, who is in you, whom you have received from God**? **You are not your own; you** were bought at a price. Therefore honor God with your body. 1 Corinthians 6:19-20 (NIV)

Having an identity with our earthly family is not a bad thing. In fact, that is how God created it, and God said that his creation was good. However, sin is not good, and the identity that we all require has been distorted and has become insufficient for us because of sin. Our family identities can even become harmful when sin is rampant in our homes.

No matter whether our homes were mostly wholesome, loving, encouraging or not, we were all raised in sinful dysfunctional families to some degree. We all have a need to identify with our heavenly Father's family and to take on the name of Christ. We are Christians. We belong to our Lord Jesus Christ. We were bought with the price of his life. And we will reign with Jesus for eternity. That is an identity that we all need, and it is the only one that fully satisfies.

Only when we take on our identity with Christ and our heavenly Father and his family can we be set free from our continual striving to find identity in various places and means here on earth.

Self-Worth in This Life

Low self-worth is a spiritual handicap. It cripples us and robs us of our ability to excel in this life. On the other hand, a truthful view of ourselves as children of God gives us the confidence we need to strive for good things in this life, to persevere and to succeed at them. A positive image of ourselves empowers us to strive for a prosperous life. In fact, a positive view of ourselves gives us the ability to see and seek positive pursuits. People with a negative view of themselves will likely succumb to something less than we could have achieved. They may do poorly in school and eventually drop out. The development of certain skills to increase their value to society may never be pursued. Dependency on others or government programs is likely. Those with a lowly view of themselves find it difficult to excel in their employment, at any level. Generally, they will see themselves as victims of others.

God created us to prosper—now and forever. Prosperity comes from God and through God, but we cut ourselves short when we believe the lie that we are worthless. We were all created by God with purpose—purpose to be a valuable member of society. Everyone has potential value. We all have different talents and abilities. Everyone is different, and we all need each other. Together we form a community and society that fits together as a living unit. Everyone has purpose. (Discussed in more detail in Chapter 6, Life Without Purpose.)

Reflection Questions

What do you think of yourself? Do you like yourself? Do you hate who you are?

How has what you have been taught from childhood formed your opinion of yourself? What lies about you have you believed about yourself?

How has the love or lack of love from your parents affected how you view yourself? How has abuse affected your personal self-worth? How has the way that you were treated lied to you about yourself?

How does knowing that God—who is love—loves you personally affect your joy?

How does knowing that God is perfecting you to become like himself affect your self-worth?

What does having the Spirit of God living within you tell you about your value to your heavenly Father as one of his children?

How is your optimistic hope affected by knowing that someday you are going to live with Jesus in his kingdom with everyone else who has been perfected in love for one another?

Describe your identity(s). Describe your drive to find identity.

What is your value to others?

Chapter 9

Setbacks

Why Is It So Hard to Be Optimistic?

When we are young, we look forward to all of the great things that will afford us just by becoming older. The five year old brags about how he is almost six. The twelve year old looks forward to becoming one year older because he will be a teenager. And then at sixteen he can get his driver's license, and he sees that his whole life will open up for him. The young look forward to the future because they are optimistic that it will get better and better as new opportunities unfold. After high school is college. And after college is a great career. And then there will be money and he can buy a new car and a house and go on trips and do all those things that he never could do before on his meager allotment of money. And then he has the hope of meeting the woman of his dreams, getting married and having his own family.

This scenario may not be the same for every person, but in general, children see growing up as having more and more freedoms, capabilities and opportunities. Life appears very long, and they cannot imagine their years that go out into their thirties, forties and on into old age.

There is a natural view that life should be a progression from one good thing to something better. For example, we hire into a company at the ground level. We work hard, but with the hope and expectation that our career will advance with promotions and raises. And the additional salary will enable us to advance our material state. We may buy a larger house, a newer car, or maybe some recreational equipment, like a boat or camper.

Life is good and advancing. Or maybe a more accurate assessment: life is good because it is advancing. At least, that is how we perceive it. We do not anticipate a setback. We have assumed all of our lives that life should progress from good to better. But what if we lose ground? What if this good life appears to have gone backward? For instance, what if that nice big house that you worked so hard for over so many years has suddenly been repossessed because of your job loss? Or, suppose you are a carpenter, but you acquired a server back injury, and now you cannot work in your trade. Now you have to start over in a new career. But now you have a wife and children to support, and a mortgage to pay off. How do you start over now?

Our natural view of life—starting from childhood—is typically one of a progression from good to better. We do not view life as filled with setbacks and the loss of what we once had. But this progressively better life is not a realistic view of life. Rarely does one proceed through life without a loss of what they once had and cherished.

At five years old, we look up to the ten year old. At ten we want to be sixteen. At sixteen we look forward to being old enough to leave home. In our twenties we see ourselves as young, good looking, free, energetic and with a glorious future. Up to this point, getting older is desirable and good. Progressing into the thirties does not seem so bad, but we joke around about always being thirty-nine year after year—as though we could halt the advancing years. Now "older" is not seen as better. Now we do not wish we were older. From this point on, as the years advance, we begin to lose our physical capabilities. Think about professional athletes. Most have to drop out of their professions by the time they are forty. Their prime is in their twenties and thirties.

Those who have chosen other careers usually peak out in their forties and fifties. And by the time they are in their sixties they are retired. They may have spent thirty to forty years advancing their career with greater income and more prestigious titles, but now they are retired, and their titles are a thing of the past, and their income is cut in half. They spent their twenties, thirties, forties and maybe fifties raising children, but now they are empty nested, and parenting has past.

In their sixties, seventies and eighties life turns around. Their health declines and their physical capabilities decline. When they were children, older meant that they could do more. Now it means that they can do less. In their twenties they were looking forward to establishing a family. Now, in the older years, their daily family life declines to just dad and mom living alone, but eventually the wife will lose her husband, or the husband will lose his wife, and she or he will be all alone. Remember when you couldn't wait to turn sixteen so you could drive. You thought about all of the freedom you would have to go places that were previously unavailable unless someone took you. Well, seventy years later you may have lost your driver's license, and now you can only go to those distant places if some younger person drives you.

Those less fortunate may have lost some of these freedoms and pleasures in younger years. They may have lost their spouse to divorce. Their dream of getting married and having a family was cut short with serious and painful relational loss that can never be replaced. And most likely, they will also experience financial and property losses that accompany divorce.

Our expectation is that life should be a continual progression of good to better, but that is not reality. Life is filled with setbacks. We will all face them with age. There are many possible setbacks in life. Sure, we all want life to just progress to bigger and better things, but that is not reality. And setbacks are great breeding ground for depression.

Biblical Examples

It does not take too much reading of the Bible to find that real life is filled with setbacks. The Bible starts out with one. Adam and Eve lived in the paradise of the Garden of Eden. It was perfect. Every need that we listed in Chapter 1 was perfectly met in this perfect existence that God created. God warned them not to partake of the tree of the knowledge of good and evil, because if they did, they would lose all that this perfect life provided. They disobeyed God, and they were banded from the garden and from the tree of life that grew there. Can you imagine how they felt? They had it all, every aspect of perfect life. And by their own foolish, disobedient and selfish choice they gave it all away. Regret could not have been greater. We have inherited our setbacks from Adam and Eve. Aging and death are a consequence of their decisions thousands of years ago. Every lacking need that we have today that promotes depression was a consequence of what they chose to give up back then when they decided to live life independent of God. *Depression is our emotional expression when we experience separation from God.*

Adam and Eve went from a perfect life to a life filled with decay. They had two sons after leaving the garden, Cain and Abel. And Cain killed Abel. How would that make you feel? Imagine having two of your own children, and one murders the other. And why did Can kill Abel? Because he was jealous of Abel's good relationship with God. A broken relationship with God will always lead us into dark places. And dark places will always rob us of joy, peace and hope.

There are many biblical character examples of men and women with setbacks; we will only look at a few.

Job's Life of Pain, Loss and Despair

Job was a righteous man who was blessed by God with a wonderful large family and a prosperous life.

There was a man in the land of Uz whose name was Job, and that man was blameless and upright, one who feared God and turned away from evil. There were born to him seven sons and three daughters. He possessed 7,000 sheep, 3,000 camels, 500 yoke of oxen, and 500 female donkeys, and very many servants, so that this man was the greatest of all the people of the east. Job 1:1-3 (ESV)

Job had done everything right in the eyes of the Lord, and the Lord blessed him. Job was content and understood that his blessings proceeded from God because of his honorable relationship with him. He did not fear a loss of life because he was a good man who depended upon God for all things. But Job was unaware that he was soon to experience a huge setback in his life. He was about to lose every earthly blessing from God, including his property, his children and even his health.

> Now the day came when the sons of God came to present themselves before the LORD—and Satan also arrived among them. The LORD said to Satan, "Where have you come from?" And Satan answered the LORD, "From roving about on the earth, and from walking back and forth across it." So the LORD said to Satan, "Have you considered my servant Job? There is no one like him on the earth, a pure and upright man, one who fears God and turns away from evil."
>
> Then Satan answered the LORD, "Is it for nothing that Job fears God? Have you not made a hedge around him and his household and all that he has on every side? You have blessed the work of his hands, and his livestock have increased in the land. But extend your hand and strike everything he has, and he will no doubt curse you to your face!" So the LORD said to Satan, "All right then, everything he has is in your power. Only do not extend your hand against the man himself!"
>
> So Satan went out from the presence of the LORD. Job 1:6-12 (NET)

Job knew his relationship with God. He knew that his blessings and protection were a consequence of living rightly before God. He had no knowledge of this conversation between God and Satan. He did not know that Satan was about to ravage his family and wealth. God was using Job as a demonstration of Job's faithfulness.

Satan came and sent enemies and storms down upon Job's possessions, servants and children, and they were all wiped out. Job was stripped bare, leaving only himself and his wife.

How would that make you feel? How would this experience affect your attitude and faith in God? Job knew that his prosperity came from God, and now he had lost it all. It did not make any sense. What a setback! How would you feel if your house burned down and all of your children were killed and all of your possessions lost? And what if you knew in your heart that you had been walking obediently with God and saw no reason for having it all taken from you? Think of all the people who have lost their homes and possession in a natural disaster, such as a hurricane, tornado, fire or tsunami as we have seen in past years.

Job was a righteous man, and he did not lose faith in God. He felt the pain of his loss, but he did not curse God.

> Then Job got up and tore his robe. He shaved his head, and then he threw himself down with his face to the ground. He said, "Naked I came from my mother's womb, and naked I will return there. The LORD gives, and the LORD takes away. May the name of the LORD be blessed!" In all this Job did not sin, nor did he charge God with moral impropriety. Job 1:20-22 (NET)

Unfortunately, for Job, the test was not finished. Satan came back to God and proclaimed that Job would not be so loyal if his health was taken from him. So God gave Satan permission to do whatever he wanted, as long as he did not take his life. So Satan attacked Job's body, but Job still did not curse God.

> So Satan went out from the presence of the LORD and afflicted Job with painful sores from the soles of his feet to the top of his head. Then Job took a piece of broken pottery and scraped himself with it as he sat among the ashes. Job 2:7-8 (NIV)

Job was now in severe pain from his sores. He was still dealing with the loss of his children, servants and possessions. And to make matters worse, his wife turned on him for not cursing God. She even suggested that he give up his life and die. But Job stands up to her and upholds God's will for his life. How would you feel in this situation?

> Then his wife said to him, "Are you still holding firmly to your integrity? Curse God, and die!" But he replied, "You're talking like one of the godless women would do! Should we receive what is good from God, and not also receive what is evil?" In all this Job did not sin by what he said. Job 2:9-10 (NET)

How would you feel if this happened to you? God has a purpose for everything, but like Job, we are not always privy to his purposes. We just see the outcome and have to deal with it as it comes. Major setbacks are always a struggle.

Many years ago God had made it clear to my wife Jo and me that we were to have as many children as he chose for us. We had nine all together. And we raised them all to know the Lord. Then, our second youngest, Abigail, was diagnosed with leukemia. What a setback! She was this beautiful, adorable ten year old, and now she had a life-threatening disease. She was put on chemotherapy for two and a half years.

When this first happened, I did not ask God, "Why me?" But I did ask him, "Why?" Over the course of the first few weeks the body of Christ poured out their love on us. They prayed, called, sent meals and blessings of many kinds. And this went on for as long as we had a need. The prayers came from people we had never met. We received letters from other states saying that their church was praying for us. I was involved in prison ministry, and the prisoners would ask about her and tell me that they had prayed for her every day.

Then the Lord revealed to me what was going on from his vantage point. He said, "Your daughter has cancer of her body. But my body (the body of Christ) has cancer too—sin. Look at the healing that is occurring in my body as a consequence of the cancer in your daughter's body." Like the situation with Job, God was fulfilling a larger objective. The challenge for us was to remain faithful to God and to continue to depend upon him, even though it may have appeared that he let us down. Actually, God was at our side the entire two and a half years of chemotherapy. We witnessed Abigail's suffering and the threat to her life due to the chemotherapy. Her blood counts were so low at times that she had no defense against infections. A blood infection would kill her within hours. There were several threats for her life during these years, but each time God came through miraculously. I can't take the time to elaborate here, but we saw the almighty hand of God in the midst of our setback. Actually, in terms of our faith in God, there was no setback. Our faiths advanced.

We never lost our precious daughter. She was ten when diagnosed with leukemia, and she is a healthy, beautiful twenty-four year old today who walks closely with our God. And she has a powerful testimony of her trial.

So how did Job fair in his setback battle? Minor setbacks that last a day or two are easy to endure and to stand against depression. But this was a major setback that by now must have gone on for several weeks, months or years with no hope in seeing things get better. Job still did not curse God, but he began to curse the fact that he even existed.

After this Job opened his mouth and cursed the day he was born. Job 3:1 (NET)

He wished that he had not been born. He wished that he could die. He was in despair over his setback. He was struggling with depression.

For the very thing I dreaded has happened to me, and what I feared has come upon me. I have no ease, I have no quietness; I cannot rest; turmoil has come upon me. Job 3:25-26 (NET)

Maybe he would have had a more optimistic attitude if he knew that God was using him as a testimony to Satan for his loyal faith to God. It still would have been very painful and disappointing, but at least he would have seen purpose for his suffering. Rarely can we see purpose for our suffering, and rarely does God make his will and purposes known to us. Like Job, in faith we just have to endure while we trust that God is using this for his purposes and that he still loves us and will bless us in the end. And that blessing may come at the end of our lives.

Job's suffering was intense, but to make matters worse, his friends came along to accuse him of sin and lack of faith. At first they consoled him, but as the suffering continued, they discouraged him with blame. Job needed encouragement, but he got the opposite. There is a lesson in this for all of us. Those who are experiencing a setback in life do not need our correction; they need our encouragement. We all suffer with depression at times, and we all need to be lifted up by those around us.

> Anxiety in a person's heart weighs him down, but an encouraging word brings him joy. Proverbs 12:25 (NET)

Encouragement is not what he found from his friend Eliphaz. Eliphaz did not know God's purposes either, but he thought he did. He accused Job as receiving the consequences of his own sin. Listen to Eliphaz's words and consider how this would make you feel in the midst of your discouragement and suffering.

> Stop and think! Do the innocent die? When have the upright been destroyed? My experience shows that those who plant trouble and cultivate evil will harvest the same. A breath from God destroys them. They vanish in a blast of his anger. Job 4:7-9 (NLT)

Then his friend counsels Job to confess his sin before God. He tries to convince him that he is just receiving God's discipline and that God is using this suffering to bless him. Eliphaz remarked,

Therefore, blessed is the man whom God corrects, so do not despise the discipline of the Almighty. For he wounds, but he also bandages; he strikes, but his hands also heal. Job 5:17-18 (NET)

But Job was a righteous man; there was nothing to confess. His friend claimed to know the will of God, but he was responding in pure ignorance. And this just added to Job's misery. There are times when we are being disciplined, and that is God's purpose. But that should not be our first assumption. In our suffering, we should always consider that God may be doing something much bigger than our own understanding. The biggest challenge is to maintain our faith in God's love for us in the midst of our suffering. We always need to live for God's will to be done for his purposes, even if we do not know them. One time, Jesus healed a blind man, and the first response from his disciples was to ask about whose sin caused his blindness, but they were in gross error.

As he went along, he saw a man blind from birth. His disciples asked him, "Rabbi, who sinned, this man or his parents, that he was born blind?"

"Neither this man nor his parents sinned," said Jesus, "but this happened **so that the work of God might be displayed in his life**. John 9:1-3 (NIV)

Our suffering may very well be "so that the work of God might be displayed in our life". And if we are not healed, it may not be because we lack faith; God's will is being accomplished. Think of this blind man. He was born blind. He grew up blind. He spent all of his life to this point blind. And this all took place so that God's glory could be revealed on one day in one small part of the world. Of course, this story has been read by millions for thousands of years. I am sure that the blind man did not see this purpose for him being born blind. Depression can come when we suffer, not knowing the purpose. Our challenge in the midst of suffering is to trust that

God has a greater purpose, and that we are honored to be chosen to fulfill his purposes.

Job's depression grew deeper, and he began to lose faith that his life had any meaning or worth in the sight of God. He saw his life as worthless, so why continue in it? He saw himself as a burden to God.

> I despise my life; I would not live forever. Let me alone; **my days have no meaning**. Job 7:16 (NIV)

> If I have sinned—what have I done to you, O watcher of men? Why have you set me as your target? **Have I become a burden to you?** Job 7:20 (NET)

Job missed the fact that his suffering life had great purpose and value in the eyes of God. Satan attacked Job's family and possessions, but possibly his greatest attack was upon his soul. Satan has the ability to plant lies such that we even accuse ourselves. Satan is the accuser (Revelation 12:10, Zechariah 3:1), and he manipulates us into a place of self-condemnation. He desires to crush our spirit with overwhelming regret. He uses our past to condemn us and pull us down. Our God is a redeemer; he buys us back from the pits of despair and depravity. So the devil draws our focus to the past and continually holds our failures before us.

Bildad was another of Job's friends, and he was of no help either. He accused Job's children for the disaster that came upon him. Like everyone else, Bildad thought that he knew God, so he assumed that he knew God's purposes. He thought he was helping Job with his vast wisdom, but his wisdom was in error—a lie.

> How long will you speak these things, seeing that the words of your mouth are like a great wind? Does God pervert justice? Or does the Almighty pervert what is right? **If your children sinned against him, he gave them over to the penalty of their sin**. But if you will look to God, and make your supplication to the Almighty, if you become pure and

upright, even now he will rouse himself for you, and will restore your righteous abode. Job 8:2-6 (NET)

How often does a sick person get accused of not having enough faith? Then these "wise prophets" quote all sorts of faith verses about healing and moving mountains. They neglect to realize that Peter tried to dissuade Jesus from going to the cross, but Jesus rebuked Satan for speaking to him through Peter. (Matthew 16:23) We all need to take caution in our "righteous" advice. Do we truly know what God is doing? We need to be cautious about what we tell others in their trials, and we need to be cautious of what we tell ourselves or what we believe from others.

This discourse between Job and his friends continues at length, but Job never comes to the truth about his situation through his friends or his own wisdom. *Job begins to see himself as unjustly cursed by God. In truth, God viewed Job as his righteous and faithful servant.* But Job saw himself before God as an unjustly, rejected enemy. He viewed his suffering as coming from the terror of God's hand against him. *He totally missed God's love for him and his high regard for his faithfulness and character.*

Only in two things spare me, O God, and then I will not hide from your face: Remove your hand far from me and stop making me afraid with your terror. Then call, and I will answer, or I will speak, and you respond to me. How many are my iniquities and sins? Show me my transgression and my sin. Why do you hide your face and regard me as your enemy? Job 13:20-24 (NET)

Job's testimony is completely against God. He blames God for everything bad. So many today curse God because of the evil that consumes the earth. Their thinking is like this: "If God is all love and if God is all powerful, then why does he allow suffering? Why does he allow evil to come upon us?" Job struggled with the same frame of mind against God. He blamed God for all that went wrong.

Surely now he has worn me out, you have devastated my entire household. You have seized me, and it has become a witness; my leanness has risen up against me and testifies against me. His anger has torn me and persecuted me; he has gnashed at me with his teeth; my adversary locks his eyes on me. People have opened their mouths against me, they have struck my cheek in scorn; they unite together against me. God abandons me to evil men, and throws me into the hands of wicked men. I was in peace, and he has shattered me. He has seized me by the neck and crushed me. He has made me his target; his archers surround me. Without pity he pierces my kidneys and pours out my gall on the ground. He breaks through against me, time and time again; he rushes against me like a warrior. Job 16:7-14 (NET)

Thus his anger burns against me, and he considers me among his enemies. His troops advance together; they throw up a siege ramp against me, and they camp around my tent. Job 19:11-12 (NET)

Pain and suffering should not be minimized. Endurance through painful trials is an ever-present battle. But the only source of victory is our reliance on God and his love for us. If our minds drift to a place of seeing God as our enemy and ourselves as his despised enemy, we will only experience defeat.

God had remained silent through all of this discourse, but in the end he spoke and set things straight. He rebuked Job for thinking that his finite wisdom could judge the purposes of God. Isn't that what we do? We try to figure things out in our lives using our own intellect, but we should be seeking out God's wisdom. The problem comes when we think that we have wisdom that God does not have. Or that our line of reasoning is higher than God's. God is the source of all wisdom. And his thoughts and ways are much higher than any of ours. (Isaiah 55:8-9) Who are we to judge God for how he decides to do anything? Is he not the creator of all things, including our lives? God rebuked and challenged Job's arrogant wisdom.

Then the LORD answered Job from the whirlwind: "Who is this that questions my wisdom with such ignorant words? Brace yourself like a man, because I have some questions for you, and you must answer them. "Where were you when I laid the foundations of the earth? Tell me, if you know so much. Who determined its dimensions and stretched out the surveying line? What supports its foundations, and who laid its cornerstone as the morning stars sang together and all the angels shouted for joy? Job 38:1-7 (NLT)

God continues his rebuke of Job's wisdom by asking him many questions regarding his knowledge of God's creation. The fear of the Lord is the beginning of our wisdom. (Job 28:28, Psalm 111:10, Proverb 1:7, 9:10, 15:33) We need to stand in awe of his power, his wisdom, his creativity, his love and compassion, his redemption and resurrection, his justice, his righteousness, his purposes and plans, and his kingdom to come. God is our only source of deliverance from anything that consumes and oppresses us. He is God and should be feared. And, as important, it is not our will that comes first, but God's. He created all things for his purposes, not ours. All of life, all of creation and all that happens in our lives are to fulfill the will of God. If we desire to walk closely with God, we need to submit to his purposes and plans. If we resist submission to him, we will only frustrate ourselves. And we will be planting the seeds of depression.

God is a loving god, and he blesses those who love him and are called according to his purposes. (Romans 8:28-39) Nothing can separate us from his love, but that does not mean that trouble and persecution will not come into our lives. Jesus is loved by his Father, and consider how God used his life for God's purposes. Why would we think that our lives are any different?

In the end, God blessed Job's life more than the first. God replaced his seven sons with seven more, and his three daughters with three more. This does not lessen the loss of his first sons and daughters, but God needed to use them for his purposes. And because he loved Job, he replaced them. He also doubled all of his material wealth.

So the LORD blessed the second part of Job's life more than the first. He had 14,000 sheep, 6,000 camels, 1,000 yoke of oxen, and 1,000 female donkeys. And he also had seven sons and three daughters. The first daughter he named Jemimah, the second Keziah, and the third Keren-Happuch. Nowhere in all the land could women be found who were as beautiful as Job's daughters, and their father granted them an inheritance alongside their brothers.

After this Job lived 140 years; he saw his children and their children to the fourth generation. And so Job died, old and full of days. Job 42:12-17 (NET)

Ruth and Naomi's Lives of Loss.

How often we plan out our lives, and we do it unaware of God's plan for our lives. We make our plans, but they do not come out the way we planned. We may have even prayed about it, but our hearts were seeking for God to fulfill our desires, not so that we could fulfill God's desires.

Life is a huge unknown. We never know what will happen in the future. So many factors are out of our control, but they affect our lives. What happens when a family member suddenly has a serious illness or accident? What happens when the economy takes a dive and you lose your job, and your wealth is depleted? What happens when your plans for a family are not met? You dreamed of marriage and family, but the years are progressing and marriage is not in sight. What happens when you planned out your career, but you couldn't open the doors needed to travel your projected path? You worked hard, saved your money, went to college, studied hard, graduated—and now you can't find a job.

When our plans do not succeed, does it occur to us that God is working out his plans? Or do we become frustrated and angry because our plans are not unfolding as we anticipated. Do we become depressed because of our failure to be in control?

In his heart a man plans his course, but the LORD determines his steps. Proverbs 16:9 (NIV)

God is fully capable of using everything in our lives for his benefit and possibly ours. He can even use our mistakes and sinful behavior. After volunteering in the prisons for many years, I have heard countless prisoners remark on how grateful they are because in prison they found God and their entire lives became new. It took prison to get their attention.

God does not look down upon the earth in frustration because things are not going according to his plans. God is not incapable of commanding his will to be done. God is aware and in control of all that happens so that his will is accomplished. Think of Jesus' life. God sent Jesus, knowing full well that we were going to reject him, lie about him, torture him, nail him to a cross and take his life. He knew ahead of time that we would do all of this out of our own sin. But God had a plan, and it was fulfilled perfectly. Now, think about our own lives. Is not God in control? Isn't he fully capable of using all of our sin and all of our mistakes for his godly outcome? He motivates us through our blessings as well as through our pain and misery. He is in control of the future of people and even nations.

The LORD foils the plans of the nations; he thwarts the purposes of the peoples. But the plans of the LORD stand firm forever, the purposes of his heart through all generations. Psalm 33:10-11 (NIV)

One definition of a setback is when we make our plans, but our plans do not turn out. How do we respond? Do we trust God for the outcomes, or do we lose hope in our lives, thinking that we are out of control, and thinking that God is not in control either.

Elimelech and his wife Naomi had two sons, Mahon and Kilion. They were Jews who lived in Bethlehem. Life may have seemed good and on track, but a famine came to the land, and their life plans were upset. They left their hometown and traveled to Moab. I suppose they felt secure because they had each other. But soon after reaching Moab, Elimelech died. That left Naomi alone with her two sons.

But then her sons married Moabite women, Orpah and Ruth. Naomi had lost her husband, but now she had her two married sons. Things went along okay for about ten years, and then her two sons died. Now there were three widow women. I am sure Naomi's life was not going according to her plan. *Setbacks are never part of our plan, but setbacks are just part of life. Actually, they are not setbacks from God's view; they are the unfolding of his plan.*

We sometime think (believe) that only pleasant things come from the Lord. We conclude that any form of loss is due to our sin or the devil or just uncontrolled chance. But God is always in control—he is God. Naomi saw her afflictions, and she did not consider them chance. She saw her life was at the hand of God.

"Don't call me Naomi," she told them. "Call me Mara, because the Almighty has made my life very bitter. I went away full, but the LORD has brought me back empty. Why call me Naomi? The LORD has afflicted me; the Almighty has brought misfortune upon me." Ruth 1:20-21 (NIV)

How do you think Naomi felt? How would you feel? It would have been easy to see your life as either forgotten by God, or as being under God's curse. How often do we pray, seeking God for deliverance or guidance, and it seems like he is nowhere to be found? We feel distraught and alone in our struggles. This is an open door for depression.

What Naomi did not realize—what we do not understand when in the midst of a miserable setback—is that God still loves us, that he is in control and that he is accomplishing something through our lives that only he understands. We need to trust him and walk in that faith. The final outcome may be that he is molding and shaping us for our own good. Or, he may be accomplishing something for his own purposes, which we are not privy to. Or it could be both. For Naomi and Ruth it was both.

Naomi and her husband had moved to Moab, but Jews were not allowed to associate with Moabites. (Deuteronomy 23:3) Remember that the territory of Moab came from Lot's oldest daughter. She got her father drunk and slept with him in order to get pregnant. Her son was Moab, the father of the Moabites. Her younger sister did the same, and her son was Ben-Ammi, the father of the Ammonites. The Moabites and Ammonites were enemies of God's people. Now Naomi's two daughter-in-laws were both Moabites. I don't think this was part of her life plan. But God had a plan. Many times our lives may seem to go astray, and we can blame it all on our own choices. We can live in regret and self condemnation. We do not want to minimize the levity of our bad choices, but if we want to be victorious, we need to know God as a loving redeemer.

God had a plan; he was making a way to redeem, not only his people, but also the gentiles. He was looking ahead thousands of years. Many times we struggle in our depression because we can only see and hope for a short distance into the future. Most of us can endure pain and disappointment for a few days and even a few months or years with the hope of being delivered and having our lives put back on a solid foundation. But what if God's plan is for the distant future, maybe beyond our lifetime? How long can we remain encouraged?

Naomi had no other choice than to return to her own people, and Ruth determined to stay at her side and return with her. Ruth may have been a Moabite, but she was also Naomi's daughter in-law by marriage.

Ruth was also a widow, and according to Jewish law, Ruth could be married by the closest family member in order to continue the family line. Such a man was called a kinsman redeemer. He redeemed the family. Boaz was a close relative to Naomi's dead husband, Elimelech, so Ruth was married to Boaz, and became part of the Jewish family. She had been a rejected Moabite, but now she was adopted into the line of Judah. And in Matthew we find the lineage of Jesus from Abraham to Joseph, the wife of Mary, mother of Jesus. In the midst of this lineage we find Ruth, the Moabite. In fact, Ruth was King David's great, great grandmother.

Salmon the father of Boaz, whose mother was Rahab, **Boaz the father of Obed, whose mother was Ruth**, Obed the father of Jesse, and Jesse the father of King David. David was the father of Solomon, whose mother had been Uriah's wife, Matthew 1:5-6 (NIV)

God had a purpose and plan. And he has a purpose and plan for each one of us. Faith is the ability to live out our lives in harmony with God's plan from our hearts and minds. It is a living walk of entrusting our lives to God, knowing that somehow God has a grand purpose for what is happening to us.

Naomi and Ruth clearly endured much loss, pain and hardship. But in the end, they were blessed by God. Setbacks can be a major cause of depression, but we must all realize that setbacks are a normal part of life, and that God may be doing something much grander than our finite perception allows for us to see. Endurance is a critical part of our battle against depression.

Apostle Paul was just a man like any one of us, and God called him to suffer for Jesus' name. Just because God calls us to do his work does not mean that our lives will be fully protected from persecution, pain and hardship. It may be just the opposite, like it was for Paul. God sent Ananias to speak to him.

But the Lord said to him, "Go, because this man is my chosen instrument to carry my name before Gentiles and kings and the people of Israel. For **I will show him how much he must suffer for the sake of my name**." Acts 9:15-16 (NET)

Paul knew that suffering was part of God's calling upon his life. And he knew that it would require great endurance over many years. He did not waver in his suffering because he knew his suffering was all part of God's purposes and plan for his life. He was strengthened in understanding what God had given him in the midst of hardship.

But as God's servants, we have commended ourselves in every way, **with great endurance, in persecutions, in difficulties, in distresses, in beatings, in imprisonments, in riots, in troubles, in sleepless nights, in hunger**, by purity, by knowledge, by patience, by benevolence, by the Holy Spirit, by genuine love, by truthful teaching, by the power of God, with weapons of righteousness both for the right hand and for the left, through glory and **dishonor, through slander** and praise; **regarded as impostors**, and yet true; as unknown, and yet well-known; **as dying** and yet—see!—we continue to live; as those who are **scourged** and yet not executed; as **sorrowful**, but always rejoicing, as poor, but making many rich, as **having nothing**, and yet possessing everything. 2 Corinthians 6:4-10 (NET)

How often do we think that God has abandoned us because we are living out a setback from our own plans for our lives? We may have concluded that if we are called by God that we would be fully protected and blessed in his work. Isn't that what many TV evangelists proclaim and project? But it doesn't take too much searching out of the Scriptures to see those Jesus called to do his work were also called to suffer. Jesus told Peter that he would have to die for him. Peter accepted this as part of God's calling upon his life. Look at what he wrote to us.

Dear friends, do not be surprised at the painful trial you are suffering, as though something strange were happening to you. But rejoice that you participate in the sufferings of Christ, so that you may be overjoyed when his glory is revealed. 1 Peter 4:12-13 (NIV)

Joseph's Life of Setbacks

When we want to travel from point to point, we try to take the shortest path. We reason that any other path would be a waste of time and resources. But God is the creator of time, and he has no limit to his resources. His paths are typically long and difficult. He can do something in a hurry, but that is rare for God. Think about his earthly creation. He has been about his work and purpose for this earthly existence for thousands of years, but we know that his eternal purposes will be accomplished upon a new earth. This one will pass away. (Isaiah 65:17, 66:22, 2 Peter 3:13, Revelation 21:1) Think of all the time and resources God is expending upon this earth that will be burned up. To us this seems like such a waste. This beautiful earthly creation and the entire universe were just temporarily created in order to accomplish a greater purpose. Think of all of the happenings of the Old Testament that were given just to point ahead to the present times, and the present times point ahead to our eternal existence. (Colossians 2:17, Hebrews 10:1)

God is not in a hurry, and he does not economize the details. He does not always take the shortest route. And when these realities become real in our lives, it can leave us frustrated and confused. We can begin to doubt and lose faith in God's hand upon our lives. Think of John the Baptist. He was clearly called by God to prepare the way of Jesus' coming. But when John was thrown into prison by Herod, he began to doubt. He asked his own disciples to ask Jesus if he was the messiah, or if there was someone else coming after him. (Matthew 11:2)

Waiting too long can bring about depression. Waiting too long can bring about doubt and confusion and disappointment. What appears as a setback to us is not a setback in God's eyes. Everything is just going according to his plan.

Let's look at the life of Joseph and what God accomplished through his setbacks. Jacob (also called Israel by God) had four wives, but Rachael was the one he treasured in his heart. Jacob had twelve sons, but only two by Rachael, Joseph and Benjamin, but Joseph was the one son he loved the most.

Joseph, being seventeen years old, was pasturing the flock with his brothers. He was a boy with the sons of Bilhah and Zilpah, his father's wives. And Joseph brought a bad report of them to their father. Now

Israel loved Joseph more than any other of his sons, because he was the son of his old age. And he made him a robe of many colors. But when his brothers saw that their father loved him more than all his brothers, they hated him and could not speak peacefully to him.

Now Joseph had a dream, and when he told it to his brothers they hated him even more. He said to them, "Hear this dream that I have dreamed: Behold, we were binding sheaves in the field, and behold, my sheaf arose and stood upright. And behold, your sheaves gathered around it and bowed down to my sheaf." His brothers said to him, "Are you indeed to reign over us? Or are you indeed to rule over us?" So they hated him even more for his dreams and for his words.

Then he dreamed another dream and told it to his brothers and said, "Behold, I have dreamed another dream. Behold, the sun, the moon, and eleven stars were bowing down to me." But when he told it to his father and to his brothers, his father rebuked him and said to him, "What is this dream that you have dreamed? Shall I and your mother and your brothers indeed come to bow ourselves to the ground before you?" And his brothers were jealous of him, but his father kept the saying in mind. Genesis 37:2-11 (ESV)

If you were Joseph at this point in his life, you would likely be thinking that life is only going to be going uphill. His father loved and blessed him more than his brothers. And God gave him two dreams revealing how he was going to someday rule over his brothers, and even his own father. Joseph had no idea how his dreams were going to come about.

Joseph's brothers hated him and were extremely jealous of his favor with their dad. Who would want to be hated by their brothers? But this was all part of God's purposes. God's plans were unfolding. This is not unlike God's own son Jesus. Jesus was hated by the Pharisees because of their jealousy. They wanted to kill him, and they did. That was also God's plan.

One day Joseph's brothers were out tending the sheep, and Isaac told him to go find them and see how they were doing. As his brothers saw him coming, they plotted to kill him. First they put him down into a dry well, where he would have had a slow death. But Judah, one of Joseph's brothers, convinced the other brothers to sell him to some Ishmaelite traders who were traveling to Egypt to sell their goods. The traders could sell him there as a slave. So Joseph was sold to Potiphar, an officer of Pharaoh, the king of Egypt. Potiphar was captain of the palace guard.

Clearly, Joseph was having a setback! He was supposed to rule over his brothers and now he was a slave in a distant land. And no one would come looking for him. His brothers lied to their father and told him a wild animal killed him. So his dad thought he was dead and his brothers had to hold to their lie. Joseph was a lonely slave in a foreign land. How do you think you would feel if you were in his situation? God promised that he would rule over his brothers, and now he was a lonely slave. Do you think that he was a setup for depression?

Well, Joseph's story gets worse. Potiphar's wife repeatedly tried to sexually seduce Joseph when her husband was gone, but Joseph repeatedly denied her requests. In her anger, she falsely accuses him of trying to seduce her. So Potiphar had Joseph thrown into prison.

Remember, God told Joseph in two dreams that he was going to rule over his brothers. This was before any of these terrible situations occurred. Can you imagine Joseph's doubt? He was spending time in prison for a crime that he did not commit. And his family was not coming to rescue him. He did not have anyone to come alongside of him. He was a prisoner, completely alone in his struggles. Imagine yourself in his predicament. How would you feel?

We don't know exactly how many years Joseph spent in prison. We do know that Joseph was seventeen when his brothers turned on him. And he was thirty when he was released from prison. His setback lasted thirteen years. That is a long time to remain optimistic, a long time to trust in the Lord's promises for him. His life seemed to be going in the exact opposite direction.

Optimism nearly always breeds encouragement followed by elation. Pessimism almost always breeds discouragement followed by depression.

Joseph's faith continued to be challenged. Two of Joseph's fellow prisoners were the Pharaoh's cupbearer and baker. Both of these men had dreams while in prison with Joseph, and Joseph interpreted each of them. And both interpretations came true. The cupbearer was restored to his position, and the baker was hanged. Joseph may have thought that here was a connection for his release. He asked these men to mention him to Pharaoh when they got out. But the baker was killed and the cupbearer forgot to mention him. And Joseph had to wait again for his unknown future to unravel. How would you feel in his situation?

Two years after the cupbearer was released from prison, the Pharaoh had two dreams. Pharaoh was troubled by them and no one could interpret them. Then the cupbearer remembered how Joseph interpreted his dreams and the baker's dreams in prison. He told Pharaoh about Joseph, who was immediately called upon. Joseph interpreted the dreams for the future of Egypt. They were to have seven good years for their crops followed by seven years of drought. Joseph recommended that Pharaoh store up grain during the seven good years in order to survive the seven drought years. Pharaoh was so impressed by Joseph that he appointed him as commander over the project. So Joseph went from a forgotten prisoner to second in command in Egypt in one day.

After thirteen years of rejection, loneliness, false accusation, slavery and imprisonment, God's dreams to Joseph came to be. During the seven years of drought, Joseph's family was running out of food, so Jacob sent Joseph's brothers to Egypt to buy some grain. The story gets rather involved at this point, but the brothers were confronted by Joseph. He was no longer the young shepherd boy that they could reject and abuse; he was second in command of Egypt. The brothers feared for their lives. Joseph could have had them all hanged or put in prison like he had been. But that is not what Joseph did. Instead, Joseph saw this entire scenario as coming from the orchestration of God Almighty.

His brothers then came and threw themselves down before him. "We are your slaves," they said.

But Joseph said to them, "Don't be afraid. Am I in the place of God? **You intended to harm me, but God intended it for good to accomplish what is now being done, the saving of many lives.** So then, don't be afraid. I will provide for you and your children." And he reassured them and spoke kindly to them. Genesis 50:18-21 (NIV)

As long as we are seeking God and obediently following his lead, we need to hold onto his love for us and his purposes for us. If we stand back, we see that it was not Joseph's purposes that were fulfilled. This entire scenario was for the fulfillment of God's purposes. I believe this story has many foretellings hidden in the story line. But Joseph clearly states, "God intended it for good to accomplish what is now being done, the saving of many lives". Many times our depression breeds from the thinking that God is for us, so our purposes should be fulfilled, but then they are not fulfilled. God does love us, and he does bless us immensely. But we must continually remember that God does not exist for us; we exist for him. God created us for his purposes, not so that we could quote his word back to him and command life to go our way. God doesn't respond to our commands. And when hardship comes, we need to endure in our faith that God is using our lives to fulfill his will.

When asked how to pray, Jesus gave us what we have coined "The Lord's Prayer", in which we pray, "Your will be done. Your kingdom come on earth as it is in heaven". Our lives are for the purposes of God's will and his kingdom. Optimism, which breeds encouragement, comes from looking at our lives as instruments of God Almighty. And if we are his children, then his purposes in and through us will result in blessings. There may be much hardship, suffering and enduring, but there will be blessings.

Jesus is the Son of God, but he became the Son of Man in order to suffer upon this earth. He suffered in order to reconcile our relationship with God. He suffered in order to defeat the devil and all evil. He suffered for the establishment of his kingdom. And at the end of all of his suffering, which included the death of his earthly body, he was raised from the dead and now sits at the right hand of God Almighty, and all authority in heaven and earth has been given to him. Jesus was used to fulfill God's purposes. He knew it. He lived it. He endured. He pursued the calling. He was not lost in his own depression. He encourages us to take the same view and attitude and to live like him in this life.

Blessed are those who are persecuted because of righteousness, **for theirs is the kingdom of heaven**.

Blessed are you when people insult you, persecute you and falsely say all kinds of evil against you because of me. Rejoice and be glad, **because great is your reward in heaven**, for in the same way they persecuted the prophets who were before you. Matthew 5:10-12 (NIV)

Setbacks from our view are not necessarily setbacks from God's view. God is just fulfilling his purposes through his plans. Job was being used by God as a witness of Job's faith in the midst of Satan's attacks upon his life. Naomi and Ruth were used by God to fulfill the salvation to the gentiles through the bloodline of Jesus. Joseph was used to deliver God's people. And Joseph is a foreshadowing of Jesus who came to deliver all of God's people from evil and the bondage of sin. Are we willing to be used by God for his righteous purposes? *Suffering is a reality in this earthly life. Victory comes, not in the deliverance of suffering, but in the truthful perspective of our suffering. God's perspective is the only truthful one. Our perspective could be a discouraging lie.*

Reflection Questions

Describe your life expectations when you were a teenager or early twenties. Did your life turn out that way, or is it turning out that way? Describe it now in comparison.

What setbacks have you experienced in your life? How did you make it through them? Did you struggle with depression? What thoughts did you struggle with?

Describe how you worked through your setback with the Lord? Did he deliver you? Did he strengthen you? Did he encourage you? How?

In your setback, did you discover God's purposes in your suffering? How did that affect your attitude? How did that affect your depression?

Chapter 10

Self-Inflicted Setbacks

In the previous chapter we talked about setbacks that were orchestrated by God. Job, Naomi, Ruth and Joseph had major setbacks that were out of their control, and they did nothing to promote these setbacks. However, it would be highly ignorant to assume that all setbacks are caused by God. Much of the time, if not most of the time, our setbacks are the consequence of our own decisions and actions. God did not put them into our lives, and, in fact, God has repeatedly warned us concerning our lives regarding how to avoid setbacks. The problem arises when we are not seeking his wisdom and counsel and then obeying his warnings and instructions. Remember, we are in this sinful state today because Adam and Eve did not adhere to God's warning not to eat of the tree of the knowledge of good and evil. We are all living in a perpetual setback due to our deficient relationship with God.

Setbacks Caused by Sin

It should be self-evident that sin destroys our lives. Jesus came to save us from our enemy of death. Death is more than biological. Our greatest enemy is spiritual death. Sin brings death, not only to our bodies, but to our inner-self, our spirit, soul and body. It brings death to all of our relationships with people and God. Sin is a killer. Many of our trials in life are brought on by ourselves. And the pain and destruction of our lives are a consequence of our own lack of godly character, our foolish ways and our own sinful desires and actions. Let's start with our personal sin. Sin is a killer. It has the power to totally destroy our lives. Ultimately, the final outcome is death. This death is more than physical; it begins with a progressive lose of our spiritual life. This is where depression lies. Depression comes from within our hearts, mind and soul. It expresses the pain of this death through the distraught feelings of depression. Our own sin is the root cause.

No one undergoing a trial should say, "I am being tempted by God." For God is not tempted by evil, and He Himself doesn't tempt anyone. But each person is tempted when **he is drawn away and enticed by his own evil desires**. Then after desire has conceived, it gives birth to sin, and **when sin is fully grown, it gives birth to death**. James 1:13-15 (HCSB)

There are countless forms and situations for sin, so let's just consider a few to get a picture of how we become the instigator for our own setbacks. Let's start with marriage setbacks.

Many experience their marriage falling apart. There is one divorce for every two marriages. Struggling marriages bring about intense emotional pain. I am sure that those who find themselves in the throes of divorce did not intend for their marriage to turn out this way when they stood at the altar professing their love for one another, exchanging rings and reciting their life-long vows to one another before God and witnesses. Now, a few years later, they are in misery and confusion and they want to escape. What happened? What went wrong? It is simple!

All—yes, all—marriage struggles are the result of sin. Marriages are between two sinners. Sin is relational. Marriage is the most intimately close relationship created by God, so sin takes its greatest toll on marriages. Not only can't we blame our marriage setbacks on God; God has provided a way of escape. God has sent Jesus so that we can conquer sin and enjoy the benefits of righteousness, peace, love and forgiveness in marriage as we seek to live out the unity in marriage as God ordained from creation.

The answer for these depressing setbacks in marriage is not to run from each other, but to run to Jesus and to obediently submit to his counsel.

However, even among proclaiming Christians, few do so. For every two Christians who vow to love their new marriage partner in the worst of situations, one of those couples refuses to maintain their vows, so they seek divorce. Divorce is filled with pain. Not only is there the pain of rejection, anger, hurt, loneliness and loss; there is the pain of a hopeless future. Marriage began with the hope of living out a life of love and fulfillment, but this hope was replaced with regret and pain and despair. And if there are children, they, too, are wounded by the failure of their parents to love each other. What started out with such high hopes of grandeur has ended in hopeless failure. Very depressing!

Hope deferred makes the heart sick, but a longing fulfilled is like a tree of life. Proverbs 13:12 (NET)

Now what? The answer for any self-induced setback is to seek out Jesus in order to redeem what was lost. He can heal you and your spouse so as to save your marriage. Pray and seek out his word. Do this together. Seek out godly counsel from those who already know and live by God's word and have demonstrated a mature walk with Jesus and a prosperous marriage.

The answer to any self-induced setback is to repent. Repentance is the conscious decision and action to turn from the way you were living to a new way that brings about life. Jesus gave a picture of repentance by describing two roads and two entrances.

Enter through the narrow gate. For the gate is wide and the road is broad that leads to destruction, and there are many who go through it. How narrow is the gate and difficult the road that leads to life, and few find it. Matthew 7:13-14 (HCSB)

I think of this as one long road with two opposing directions. Repentance is the decision and act of turning from the wide, easy direction that leads to destruction to the other direction that is narrow and hard, but leads to true life. In this parable, Jesus is the gate to life, and Jesus is the way to travel.

Jesus told him, "I am the way, the truth, and the life. No one comes to the Father except through Me. John 14:6 (HCSB)

Then Jesus spoke to them again: "I am the light of the world. Anyone who follows Me will never walk in the darkness but will have the light of life." John 8:12 (HCSB)

I am the gate; whoever enters through me will be saved. He will come in and go out, and find pasture. The thief comes only to steal and kill and destroy; I have come that they may have life, and have it to the full. John 10:9-10 (NIV)

Repentance is the giving up of our old life in order to live a new life through Jesus Christ. We used to belong to the devil and his ways of living. The thief in the previous passage is the devil, who comes to "steal and kill and destroy". Jesus came that we would have abundant life. But we cannot live both ways with both the devil and Jesus as our master. Repentance is the conscious act of choosing who will be our master; the devil, the world and our evil nature, or to follow Jesus, who is the essence of true life. Jesus offers his Spirit to live within us. He has also given us his written word to instruct us and to give us his very own promises for our lives. Repentance requires of us to lose our old life in order to have a new one by his Spirit and his word.[6]

---

[6] We are powerless over sin without the Spirit of Christ living within us. (Romans 8:1-17, Galatians 5:13-6:10) All that we need to do is ask to receive his Spirit for the heartfelt intent of living a new life in Jesus Christ. (Luke 11:13) And our thinking needs to be changed. The written word of God has been given to us so that our

For whoever wants to save his life will lose it, but whoever loses his life because of Me will find it. What will it benefit a man if he gains the whole world yet loses his life? Or what will a man give in exchange for his life? Matthew 16:25-26 (HCSB)

Life is a series of choices. We choose life or death by the way we choose to travel. It is a choice. God does not make it for us. But he does call us to make the right choice and have life.

Today I have given you the choice between life and death, between blessings and curses. Now I call on heaven and earth to witness the choice you make. Oh, that you would choose life, so that you and your descendants might live! You can make this choice by loving the LORD your God, obeying him, and committing yourself firmly to him. This is the key to your life. And if you love and obey the LORD, you will live long in the land the LORD swore to give your ancestors Abraham, Isaac, and Jacob." Deuteronomy 30:19-20 (NLT)

In one sense, because it is our choice to walk in the ways of life or the ways of death, it is also our choice to sow the seeds of depression or the seeds of joy. But we cannot expect joy if we are sowing to the destructive ways of our sinful nature.

Let's look at addictions for another example of our sinful nature so we can understand how sin can destroy our lives. Addictions are another major contributor to a destroyed life. Alcohol, drugs, pornography, overeating, gambling, smoking and several others—they all have the inevitable ability to rob us of life. They have the power to ruin our careers, our marriages, our finances, our health, our view of ourselves and—most catastrophic—our relationship with God. Addictions don't start out looking so deathly.

---

thinking can be transformed. We all need to be reading and studying God's word, the Bible. (Romans 12:1-2, 2 Timothy 3:16-17)

Initially, they seem to relieve our anxieties and life stresses. But as James wrote (above), "after desire has conceived, it gives birth to sin, and when sin is fully grown, it gives birth to death". Once trapped, it seems nearly impossible to escape. The fruit of addictions is a loss of true life. One addiction can be complicated with several others. For example, it is not uncommon for gambling, alcohol, drugs and smoking to have captured the same person. On the flipside, it only takes one addiction to destroy several aspects of one's life. For example, an alcohol addiction can destroy one person's marriage, employment, health, finances, self-worth and relationship with God.

The pursuit of an addiction may begin with the hope of satisfaction and deliverance from the trials of life, but in the end, the struggles increase with no hope of escape. When hope is depleted, depression overshadows all of life. Our life has taken on a serious setback, and we have no one to blame but ourselves. And once we realize that, we can become even more hopelessly depressed. We have stepped into a pit, and now we see no way to escape.

Let's consider one more area where sin can bring about a major life setback. Sin can destroy our careers and employment opportunities. What if you are a complainer? What if you are lazy? What if you are irresponsible? What if you come in late, leave early and take long breaks? What if you are unproductive and waste time at work? What if you do not get along with your boss, fellow employees or subordinates? What if you are dishonest? What if you are self-seeking and do not seek the benefits of others or the company as a whole? All of these qualities can rob us of a successful, prosperous and joyful career. Many hate their job and hate to go to work; and whose fault is that? A bad attitude and poor character will plant the seeds of a poor career and may even result in becoming fired. Who's to blame? We all need to work to supply our daily needs, and for personal joy and satisfaction, but our sinful behavior can destroy it all. Hating our job, being passed up for advancement, lacking affirmation and possibly losing our job can lead to deep depression and hopelessness. Those who fail at employment due to their own shortcomings in character typically find themselves failing at one job after another. They are left hopeless and depressed. And the destruction usually does not end at the job. The anger, anxiety, hurt and the pain of failure usually come home and infect the entire family. It pervades every aspect of life. Life appears to be a downward spiral, and depression can consume us.

These sin produced setbacks have the potential for depression just as setbacks that God brings about in our lives. And the answer for victory over depression is about the same. If we seek God's will and walk in his will, we can overcome. More will be said about this victory throughout this book.

Setbacks Caused by a Lack of Godly Character

We have already discussed how ungodly character can destroy one's career. And it should be recognized that anything that is ungodly is not too distant from becoming sinful. But let's focus on the lack of godly character and the negative consequences that can bring about setbacks in our lives. Ungodly character is not that unlike our sinful nature, but with a different focus. The understanding of character focuses more on who we are than our outward actions. However, our character always expresses itself through our actions. Let's consider a few examples. Let's start with laziness. If I was to lay around all day watching TV, accomplishing nothing productive, it is not obvious that I have sinned or done anything wrong. But I have not exhibited godly character. So how might laziness cause a self-induced setback? One day of laziness probably would not, but if my character was laziness, it would likely be exhibited continuously. It may not be that I would lay in bed all day watching TV. I may even have a job, but because of my laziness, I may only do what is absolutely required. At home it may be that I don't change the engine oil of my car or maintain my house. In regards to my health, I may not exercise and eat healthy. What would that do to my life? Solomon summed it up quite well.

I walked by the field of a lazy person, the vineyard of one with no common sense. I saw that it was overgrown with nettles. It was

156

covered with weeds, and its walls were broken down. Then, as I looked and thought about it, I learned this lesson: A little extra sleep, a little more slumber, a little folding of the hands to rest—then poverty will pounce on you like a bandit; scarcity will attack you like an armed robber. Proverbs 24:30-34 (NLT)

The one who is lazy becomes poor, but the one who works diligently becomes wealthy. Proverbs 10:4 (NET)

We all have physical needs. We need food to eat, a place to live, clothing, transportation, and many other provisions for our lives. In order to provide for ourselves; we need to get out and work. Laziness has the power to rob us of blessings. Not only can we lose our property, we can lose our self-esteem and confidence in life. Laziness can lead to one setback after another. Lazy people likely drive old, high mileage cars, cars that are not very dependable, cars that unexpectedly surprise us with costly repairs. I have known lazy people who did not check their oil level, and consequently "burned up" their engine due to low oil. Laziness is nearly guaranteed to bring about very discouraging and stressful setbacks.

Paul gave strong instructions for dealing with lazy people in the church of God's people. He also made a strong argument that we all need to be a people who diligently work hard in order to maintain a good reputation for those of the world who look at Christians and their lives.

For even when we were with you, we gave you this rule: "If a man will not work, he shall not eat." 2 Thessalonians 3:10 (NIV)

Make it your ambition to lead a quiet life, to mind your own business and to work with your hands, just as we told you, so that your daily life may win the respect of outsiders and so that you will not be dependent on anybody. 1 Thessalonians 4:11-12 (NIV)

If you want to escape depression, I suggest that you become productive. Even if you are not lazy, being productive is a good discipline in your battle against depression. Don't just lay around in seclusion; get out and do something that is of benefit to yourself and others. Even if you do not earn money, help someone else that is in need with what God has given you. Being productive and serving others is powerful medicine for deliverance from depression.

Let's consider pride. Pride comes from the heart of man. It is an inner character quality that flows from us like a polluted river, but when we look at ourselves, we see the water as sparkling clean and refreshing. Pride is the inner opinion that we are somehow better than others. We may think of our self as more intelligent and always right. We may consider our self wealthy, and therefore above others. We may think of our self better looking, and therefore more appealing to others. We may be a high achiever and more successful and therefore see our self as being of a higher status as compared to others. We may see our self as more righteous, and therefore closer to God than the lowly sinner. Pride is living out a lie about our self. It is viewing our self as being much more than what we truthfully are in the eyes of God.

So how can pride bring us down? Prideful people think that others look up to them, but in reality, they are a disgrace.

Pride leads to disgrace, but with humility comes wisdom. Proverbs 11:2 (NLT)

We were all created to need the love and appreciation of others. We need people in our lives because we were created in the image of God as relational beings. Relationships are delicate. It is easy to destroy them. Pride is one of those relationship destroyers. It begins by destroying our own healthy view of others. Instead of thinking highly of others, we think and act as though others are lowly, while we portray ourselves as above them. The net effect is separation, rejection and avoidance by others.

So how does this work? We all struggle in our relationships. That is because we all struggle with sin and we all lack the perfect character of God. Another description of pride is arrogance. Arrogance portrays an attitude that we are better than others. We may think that our "superiority" will raise the opinions of others for us, but instead it causes offense. No one wants a friend that looks down at them. No one wants a friend that believes he is better than us. Arrogance is offensive. Arrogance is poor character. The following proverbs attest to these facts.

Arrogance leads to nothing but strife, but wisdom is gained by those who take advice. Proverbs 13:10 (HCSB)

Pride goes before destruction, and a haughty spirit before a fall. It is better to be lowly in spirit with the afflicted than to share the spoils with the proud. Proverbs 16:18-19 (NET)

Mockers are proud and haughty; they act with boundless arrogance. Proverbs 21:24 (NLT)

Pride ends in humiliation, while humility brings honor. Proverbs 29:23 (NLT)

Rarely will you find depression among someone who has many loving, caring and intimate friends. Love for others and the love from others is a cure for almost any struggle. But on the flipside, many think that friendship entails having others look up to us. This is common among teenagers. Many of them struggle to be the coolest in order to win friends. They are in a continual pursuit of impressing others in order to be accepted and included and raised up. They are practicing arrogance.

Adults practice arrogance as well, but we are more sophisticated—at least, in our pride, we think we are more sophisticated. Our supposed superiority is "hidden" in job titles, expensive possessions, achievements, the things we do, our knowhow, how we look, our ability to impress and any other means of comparison where we can excel above others.

This rat-race of relational competition for acceptance and gaining friends can be an endless and disappointing pursuit. There are two ends of the spectrum. There are those who stand out as superior—at least they think they do. And then there are those who think they are the least in the eyes of others. Both groups are unsatisfied because arrogant superiority is just a façade and does not foster close friendships. Some of the most popular and wealthy people commit suicide. Reasons for suicide vary, but without close, loving relationships, anyone is in danger of hopeless depression. Money, fame and success do not foster these intimate relationships with others that are basic to our sanity and having an abundant life. The key to having real and close friendships is not prideful superiority. It is being humble and loving. It is in raising others up rather than ourselves. Jesus is our example.

Don't be selfish; don't try to impress others. Be humble, thinking of others as better than yourselves. Don't look out only for your own interests, but take an interest in others, too.

You must have the same attitude that Christ Jesus had. Though he was God, he did not think of equality with God as something to cling to. Instead, he gave up his divine privileges; he took the humble position of a slave and was born as a human being. When he appeared in human form, he humbled himself in obedience to God and died a criminal's death on a cross. Philippians 2:3-8 (NLT)

Do not seek your own good, but the good of the other person. 1 Corinthians 10:24 (NET)

Jesus did not try to impress anyone for their approval. In fact, he offended many prideful people (mostly the Pharisees who saw themselves as far above others, including Jesus because of his popularity, authority and power). He offended them to the point of being persecuted and eventual death at the hands of his enemies. But the friendships that he did have were rich and deep. And the key to these deeper relationships was not what other did for Jesus, but what Jesus did for others. He lived—and died—for others. We don't need to be held in high regard by everyone. We need to be humble and loving. Then we will be held in high regard by Jesus. Then we will be held in high regard by others who are humble. And lastly we will be held in high regard by the prideful, but that may never occur because they do not want to lose their place by lowering themselves down.

Character can bring us down or it can raise us up. Godly character is always humble, but ironically, humility will raise us up. A lack of godly character can induce all sorts of setbacks in our lives—self-induced setbacks. Seeking God for his character is a strong defense against depression.

Let's be honest and real; this life is a struggle for all of us. We all live in a fallen world. It is fallen because of our own character and behaviors. It is a struggle to become like Jesus, who is perfect. But even Jesus was made perfect in his suffering and struggles.

> For it was fitting that he, for whom and by whom all things exist, in bringing many sons to glory, should make the founder of their salvation perfect through suffering. Hebrews 2:10 (ESV)

> Although he was a son, he learned obedience through the things he suffered. Hebrews 5:8 (NET)

We should not be discouraged or depressed when we suffer the many trials that life can bring, even when being rejected by others. For suffering develops godly character, and that is what we all need.

> Not only this, but we also rejoice in sufferings, knowing that suffering produces endurance, and endurance, character, and character, hope. And hope does not disappoint, because the love of God has been

poured out in our hearts through the Holy Spirit who was given to us.
Romans 5:3-5 (NET)

It is foolish to endlessly try to impress others with our bad character.
Some even think that bragging about our corrupted character will win
friends. Many will foolishly brag about how drunk they got, how high they
got, how many sexual affairs they had and many other deviant behaviors.
And while they hang out with each other—all trying to impress each
other—they only succeed in becoming worse.

Do not be misled: "Bad company corrupts good character." Come back
to your senses as you ought, and stop sinning; for there are some who
are ignorant of God—I say this to your shame. 1 Corinthians 15:33-34
(NIV)

So don't be so concerned about what the worldly think of you. Seek
God's approval. Hang with those who are also seeking the same. You might
find a group of friends that truly satisfy. Remember: Good character is
highly valuable, and it has the power to bring joy and peace.

Setbacks Caused by Foolishness

Many of our setbacks are self-induced by our own foolish choices and
behaviors. Sin, foolishness and poor character usually go together, but let's
focus on the aspect of foolishness.

What is foolishness? To be foolish is opposite of being wise. *Wisdom is
the ability to see and understand the truth about life and all that occurs.
Wisdom forms a strong foundation for life—assuming that we walk in that
wisdom.* Foolishness is typically borne by the prideful. They think they
know all, but in reality they are blind to the truth. God is all wisdom and
truth. That is why the psalmist defined the fool as one who does not
believe in God.

The fool says in his heart, "God does not exist." They are corrupt, and they do vile deeds. There is no one who does good. God looks down from heaven on the human race to see if there is one who is wise, one who seeks God. All have turned away; all alike have become corrupt. There is no one who does good, not even one. Psalm 53:1-3 (HCSB)

Wisdom comes from God. And God has given Jesus to us, who has become our infinite flow of wisdom and strength. The secret to becoming wise is to seek wisdom from God.

If any of you lacks wisdom, he should ask God, who gives generously to all without finding fault, and it will be given to him. James 1:5 (NIV)

There is a paradox regarding fools and the wise. The cure for foolishness is to become wise. But a fool, by nature, does not seek wisdom. It is like they are in a trap with no escape. If they could only see that God is the only source of life. For without him, there is no such thing as life, for God defines life; God is life. It is impossible to obtain life without being obediently connected to him. The fool believes he can find and obtain life on his own. And maybe that defines a fool, someone who thinks he can live without God.

The fear of the LORD is the beginning of knowledge, but fools despise wisdom and discipline. Proverbs 1:7 (NIV)

He who trusts in himself is a fool, but he who walks in wisdom is kept safe. Proverbs 28:26 (NIV)

There are countless downfalls of the foolish. Let's look just a few to get a picture. Let's start with the foolish use of money. Most people desire more money, but the fool does not know how to handle money wisely. So he is always lacking and rarely prospers.

Of what use is money in the hand of a fool, since he has no intention of acquiring wisdom? Proverbs 17:16 (NET)

Fools do not know how to spend money wisely. They do not know how to save and invest. And they are typically a slave to borrowing money from those who have wisely saved and invested.

The rich rule over the poor, and the borrower is servant to the lender. Proverbs 22:7 (NIV)

The fool does not save for what he desires. Rather, he borrows the money with interest, and then pays nearly twice as much for his purchase. In effect, he foolishly cuts his purchasing power in half. And the lender— who was disciplined and wise enough to save—doubles his purchasing power at the hand of the fool.

Fools seek short-term pleasures and forgo long-term gains. This is true in all areas of life, not just money. They are prone to taking the wrong paths in life because these paths look delightful at the moment, but they are not looking ahead with the sight of wisdom. For example, someone may forgo developing skills that will bless him for the rest of his life. And he becomes blind-sighted by a $15 per hour job that he can get today with his high school education. He cannot see into the future. He does not think about future job satisfaction, job opportunities, supplying the needs that come with increasing responsibilities, such as having a family. He does not seek out wise counsel; he thinks he already can see everything from his own vantage point. He convinces himself by hanging with other fools who agree with his foolish choices. He is destined for a troubled life, but he cannot see it. He surrounds himself with those who will tell him what he wants to hear.

A fool finds no pleasure in understanding but delights in airing his own opinions. Proverbs 18:2 (NIV)

Walk with the wise and become wise; associate with fools and get in trouble. Proverbs 13:20 (NLT)

Blessings come by surrounding one's self with the wise and avoiding those who are foolish. But fools have a tendency to hang with one another. The wise seek God for wisdom and then walk in that wisdom. God is the only source of true life blessings, so the wise seek God daily.

How blessed is the one who does not follow the advice of the wicked, or stand in the pathway with sinners, or sit in the assembly of scoffers! Instead he finds pleasure in obeying the LORD's commands; he meditates on his commands day and night. He is like a tree planted by flowing streams; it yields its fruit at the proper time, and its leaves never fall off. He succeeds in everything he attempts. Not so with the wicked! Instead they are like wind-driven chaff. For this reason the wicked cannot withstand judgment, nor can sinners join the assembly of the godly. Certainly the LORD guards the way of the godly, but the way of the wicked ends in destruction. Psalm 1:1-6 (NET)

The wise seek counsel from those with more wisdom, and then they wisely seek the ways of the wise.

I did not come to know and follow the Lord until I was twenty-nine years old. So I had many years to sow the seeds of fools. I drank, I gave up my virginity. In fact, it was my aim to sleep with all the women I could. Foolishly I concluded that if we were consensual, who did it hurt? I could not see ahead to how my addiction would affect my eventual marriage. I did not consider the possibility of producing a child out-of-wedlock that would spend his life without his father (me). It was easy to continue down the road of fools because there were so many other fools going in the same direction—men and women. Even after I was married, I did not see that the road I traveled was headed for destruction. I was a vulgar, selfish individual who sought out fleshly pleasure, unaware of the consequences.

I was the source of my own eventual life setbacks that likely included divorce, but the Lord was gracious. My wife went to church, but I had been that route and refused to go with her. Then, after a few years, she invited me to a Bible study at her church. I decided to go, and I bought a newer Bible translation for the class. I went, and argued with the instructor each time. After three times, she called me up and said, "I think it would be best if you didn't come anymore." She kicked me out of her class.

My wife was disappointed, but God was in control. He had a plan, and I was walking in it. I decided to read my new Bible while Jo went to church on Sunday. During this time Jesus led me in his word and sent his Spirit to open my eyes. I became wise and my whole direction of life changed. But I was so close to losing it all. I was a fool whom God made wise, and I am still growing in his wisdom. Without it, life setbacks are inevitable.

There are countless scenarios regarding the pitfalls of fools. We all have our stories. We all know of others who have suffered from their own doings. Eventually, we come to know that we are our own worst enemy. We lose our self-esteem. We feel lost, hopeless and distraught. And depression flows in like a dark cloud.

Is there any hope? God is our only hope. That is why he sent Jesus. Jesus came to change who we are. He came to give us a new heart. He came to transform our thinking and attitudes. He came to give us a whole new life. The devil is a thief, and he has already been working to rob us of all life. Jesus came to rescue us from his grip and to give us an abundant life.

The thief comes only to steal and kill and destroy; I have come so that they may have life, and may have it abundantly. John 10:10 (NET)

He delivered us from the power of darkness and transferred us to the kingdom of the Son he loves, Colossians 1:13 (NET)

Out of his love for us, he leads us into repentance, which is a pursuit of his life—eternal life. This is our only hope. All else is a "chasing after the wind". The wind is never caught, and depression is caught instead.

Repentance, the Key to Hope

We cannot change our past. Many times depression is founded on the regrets of our past. We may have formed many destructive roots. We may have allowed those roots to sprout and defile our lives. There may be no one else responsible for what we have done to our lives, and our lives may still be on the same destructive path. So what hope do we have? Hopelessness breeds depression. And depression depletes us of encouragement and motivation. We can enter an endless spiral that leads into deeper and darker despair and depression. Who will save us? Who will rescue us from this peril that has taken us captive?

The answer is Jesus, but that can sound so trite. And it is, if that is all that is said. There is a preparation for Jesus, and we must prepare. Before Jesus came to this earth, God sent John the Baptist to prepare the way for Jesus' coming. The preparation was quite simple; he called people to repentance.

> In those days John the Baptist came to the Judean wilderness and began preaching. His message was, "Repent of your sins and turn to God, for the Kingdom of Heaven is near." The prophet Isaiah was speaking about John when he said, "He is a voice shouting in the wilderness, 'Prepare the way for the LORD's coming! Clear the road for him!'" Matthew 3:1-3 (NLT)

What is repentance? Too often repentance is seen as the warning of a curse if we do not stop sinning. It is true that if we do not turn from our sinful ways that our sinful ways will bring about destruction; it will be inevitable. As this may be true, the call to repentance should be seen as an encouraging call to pursue life rather than destruction. The focus is on the pursuit of life. John the Baptist was not sent to call down curses on sinners. He came to prepare the way for Jesus. Jesus is life—true life. John was sent to prepare the way of life for us all. Jesus gave a picture of this road of repentance.

> Enter through the narrow gate. For the gate is wide and the road is broad that leads to destruction, and there are many who go through it. How narrow is the gate and difficult the road that leads to life, and few find it. Matthew 7:13-14 (HCSB)

Jesus describes this as two roads, one that leads to destruction and one that leads to life. I like to think of this as one road with two directions. The road is our life. We are all on this road at some place. The direction we are traveling is much more critical than where we are on the road. Our hope and encouragement is much more dependent upon our direction than our location on the road. To repent is simply to change direction. We turn from a life of destruction to the road of life. We turn from walking away from God to walking toward God. We turn from a sinful and destructive life to a life of righteousness. Righteousness can be thought of as anything we do or think that brings about true life.

> In the path of righteousness there is life, but another path leads to death. Proverbs 12:28 (NET)

> He who pursues righteousness and love finds life, prosperity and honor. Proverbs 21:21 (NIV)

This call to repentance is actually a call to come out of our old life that is sapping the life out of us. It is a call to seek out the creator of life, who desires to freely give us his life if we will just pursue it. That is the call to repentance. It is a call to flee from sin that gives birth to death and to live for righteousness that gives birth to life.

The entire Bible is a call to life, but let's just focus on a few of Paul's words on sin versus righteousness.

For the sin of this one man, Adam, **caused death to rule** over many. But even greater is **God's wonderful grace and his gift of righteousness, for all who receive it will live in triumph over sin and death through this one man, Jesus Christ.**

Yes, Adam's one sin brings condemnation for everyone, but Christ's one act of righteousness **brings a right relationship with God and new life for everyone.** Because one person disobeyed God, many became sinners. But because one other person obeyed God, many will be made righteous.

God's law was given so that all people could see how sinful they were. But as people sinned more and more, God's wonderful grace became more abundant. So just as sin ruled over all people and brought them to death, now God's wonderful grace rules instead, giving us right standing with God and resulting in eternal life through Jesus Christ our Lord. Romans 5:17-21 (NLT)

In the same way, count yourselves dead to sin but alive to God in Christ Jesus. **Therefore do not let sin reign in your mortal body so that you obey its evil desires. Do not offer the parts of your body to sin, as instruments of wickedness, but rather offer yourselves to God, as those who have been brought from death to life; and offer the parts of your body to him as instruments of righteousness. For sin shall not be your master, because you are not under law, but under grace.** Romans 6:11-14 (NIV)

When you were slaves to sin, you were free from the control of righteousness. What benefit did you reap at that time from the things you are now ashamed of? **Those things result in death!** But now that **you have been set free from sin and have become slaves to God, the benefit you reap leads to holiness, and the result is eternal life.** For the wages of sin is death, but the gift of God is eternal life in Christ Jesus our Lord. Romans 6:20-23 (NIV)

In these verses, Paul is describing repentance. He is saying that Jesus came so that his "grace might reign through righteousness". (Romans 5:21 NIV) Jesus came to free us from the slavery of sin so that we might become slaves of righteousness. (Romans 6:1-23) This is repentance. We turn from death by turning from sin, and we turn toward life by turning toward righteousness.

This is the great hope that we have from God through Jesus Christ. Sin is destroying us. It is robbing us of the essence of life. Jesus came so that we would have his power over sin and his power to live righteously so that we could flee death and obtain life—his life—eternal life. This is repentance. This is what it means to be truly saved. This is what it means to belong to Christ Jesus.

See how very much our Father loves us, for he calls us his children, and that is what we are! But the people who belong to this world don't recognize that we are God's children because they don't know him. Dear friends, we are already God's children, but he has not yet shown us what we will be like when Christ appears. **But we do know that we will be like him, for we will see him as he really is. And all who have this eager expectation will keep themselves pure, just as he is pure**.

Everyone who sins is breaking God's law, for all sin is contrary to the law of God. And you know that **Jesus came to take away our sins**, and there is no sin in him. **Anyone who continues to live in him will not sin.** But anyone who keeps on sinning does not know him or understand who he is.

Dear children, don't let anyone deceive you about this: **When people do what is right, it shows that they are righteous, even as Christ is righteous**. But when people keep on sinning, it shows that they belong to the devil, who has been sinning since the beginning. But **the Son of God came to destroy the works of the devil. Those who**

have been born into God's family do not make a practice of sinning, because God's life is in them. So they can't keep on sinning, because they are children of God. So now we can tell who are children of God and who are children of the devil. **Anyone who does not live righteously and does not love other believers does not belong to God.** 1 John 3:1-10 (NLT)

Remember the roads that Jesus described—one leading to a destructive life and the other leading to his abundant life. In this life we are pilgrims traveling on this road. If we have come to Christ and received his Spirit, we are someplace on this road headed toward life. But we have not reached the end yet; we have not reached the final fulfillment. But we are headed in that direction. And the farther we travel on this road, the more of his abundant life we experience. This is our hope; not that we have already obtained all that God has promised, but that we are gaining more and more each day as we press forward on the journey. And we have the hope of one day seeing Jesus face-to-face, and then we will be instantly changed into his likeness, and then we will be completely righteous with not one shred of sin that had been destroying us. God looks at this hope that we have of becoming completely like Jesus, and he sees in us his purification of our hearts.

This is a joyous pursuit. And it is a key to overcoming our hopeless and depressing view of our lives.

Reflection Questions

How much of your discouragement is due to how your actions have destroyed your life? Describe your situation and how it makes you feel. What sins do you need to repent of? How have those sins affected your life?

How has your character been a detriment to your life? Describe your character and how it has affected your relationships and your employment opportunities.

What foolish choices, decisions, thinking, attitudes or actions have had a negative effect on your life?

What in your life do you need to turn from, and what do you need to pursue instead? Be specific. Do not just say, "Follow Jesus." What are you going to stop doing and what are you going to start doing?

Chapter 11

Struggle Against Regret

Regret is living in the pain of past mistakes. We cannot go back and fix them, yet our past affects the present and the future. For example, suppose that you started a business. You borrowed a large sum of money. Maybe you got a second mortgage on your house. And possibly you gave up a secure career in a corporation in order to venture out on your own. But regretfully, after spending many long hours and years working to succeed, your business venture failed. And over those years, you lost many valuable hours with your children because you were at work. And your marriage struggled under the stress. Now you are left empty, as though you had been ravaged by a thief. You have lost money, a career, a livelihood, and relationships with your children, and your marriage is not good. And you feel like a foolish failure. You cannot go back and change your past, but now you must live with the consequences. Dwelling on your past mistakes and failures feeds depression.

Regrets come in numerous varieties and the examples are endless. Maybe you hung out with the wrong friends when you were young and together became addicted to alcohol or drugs. Now your life is ravaged and in despair. Maybe you got your girlfriend pregnant and now you are forced to make some life-long decisions. Maybe she got an abortion and you are dealing with the guilt and loss. Maybe you did not take school seriously, and now you are older and struggling to make a living—wishing you had pursued a career like many of your friends who are now prospering. Maybe you got started on smoking when you were young, and now you are old with emphysema and an oxygen tube fixed to your nostrils. Maybe you got caught up in porn and in time ruined your marriage. Maybe you violated a law by violating someone and now you are in prison. Maybe—maybe— maybe! We all have regrets. We all live apart from God by some measure and by some means.

Does God know how we feel? Think about it. God created the entire universe. He created the earth and filled it with living vegetation, sea creatures, animals and mankind. It abounded with life! And he gave it to man to rule over it and cause it to prosper as under God. He created man in his own image so that he could have a living relationship with us, and so that we could have rich, loving relationships with one another. This was a glorious creation. It was vast, holy and righteous, and it abounded in the riches of life that proceeded from this perfect relationship with God. Everything was good, and God found great joy in it.

But this wonderful existence in the paradise of God all came to an end when mankind rebelled against God. Evil increased with each generation, and it was not very long when the pain that God endured brought him to a decision to destroy nearly all living creatures and start over with Noah and his family. God grieved that he had made man and all living creatures.

The LORD saw how great man's wickedness on the earth had become, and that every inclination of the thoughts of his heart was only evil all the time. The LORD was **grieved** that he had made man on the earth, and his **heart was filled with pain**. So the LORD said, "I will wipe mankind, whom I have created, from the face of the earth—men and animals, and creatures that move along the ground, and birds of the air—for **I am grieved that I have made them**." Genesis 6:5-7 (NIV)

God was clearly experiencing emotional pain over his creation. He had not created mankind to be evil and wicked. He created us to flourish in life. But all of life proceeds from God, and his created beings rejected him and foolishly chose to seek life without him. God was grieved and it hurt. Translators have struggled to properly describe what God was feeling at this time. As referenced here in the NIV, the Lord was "grieved" that he had made man, and his "heart was filled with pain". The NET version says that the Lord "regretted" creating man and that he was "highly offended". The ESV and NKJV translations say that the Lord was "sorry" for making mankind and that it "grieved him to his heart". The HCSB says that the Lord "regretted" his creation and was "grieved in his heart". The NLT translation says that the Lord was "sorry" that he made man and that it "broke his heart". God obviously felt great pain in his heart over the waywardness of mankind, which he had created.

God had created mankind to live in righteousness and love, and so to live in peaceful harmony with him forever. He created us for his pleasure, and we, too, would find great pleasure in this harmonious relationship with God and one another. But mankind chose a different path of wickedness that brought about destruction and separation from God. God had already reduced their lifespan from nearly a thousand to 120 years. And now he was going to destroy all of mankind and animals that he created with a flood—saving only Noah, his family and the animals upon the ark that he would have Noah build. God knows the pain of regret!

God destroyed mankind with the flood, saving just Noah and his family. But that did not put an end to man's wickedness. Evil is still rampant upon the earth today. The Church is filled with sin—blatant sin, and it should not be so. The Holy Spirit was sent to restore us. John was very clear when he wrote,

Everyone who sins breaks the law; in fact, sin is lawlessness. But you know that he appeared so that he might take away our sins. And in him is no sin. **No one who lives in him keeps on sinning. No one who continues to sin has either seen him or known him**.

Dear children, do not let anyone lead you astray. He who does what is right is righteous, just as he is righteous. He who does what is sinful is of the devil, because the devil has been sinning from the beginning. **The reason the Son of God appeared was to destroy the devil's work. No one who is born of God will continue to sin, because God's seed remains in him; he cannot go on sinning, because he has**

been born of God. This is how we know who the children of God are and who the children of the devil are: Anyone who does not do what is right is not a child of God; nor is anyone who does not love his brother. 1 John 3:4-10 (NIV)

So how do you think God feels today? He regretted creating mankind in the days of Noah because "every inclination of the thoughts of his heart was only evil all the time". Has mankind changed? Even in his Church, what pain does he endure over the willful, wayward sins of his own Church? This is the pain of the cross. We hung him on the cross. It was our sin that he felt, then and now. God did not create us to live as we do. He warned Adam and Eve, but they chose to believe the devil instead; they believed the lie that God must have been selfishly deceiving them. How do you think God felt about his creation then? How do you think he feels about it now? He has to deal with and endure the pain of our waywardness from his original intent and design.

God knows perfectly well how we feel when we have to live with the pain of our past decisions and choices.

But also realize that God is not enduring the pain without the joy of the future. Jesus suffered this pain that we have been describing with the joy of what was going to happen as a consequence.

Let us fix our eyes on Jesus, the author and perfecter of our faith, who **for the joy set before him endured the cross**, scorning its shame, and sat down at the right hand of the throne of God. Hebrews 12:2 (NIV)

Regret without hope is depression. Regret with hope may mean that we have to endure the pain of our present situations, but not without a future victory for focus. A future focus is the key to our hope.

How do we get this hope? What is it? What does it look like and how does it work? Can we live with a victorious attitude on the inside when our lives are weighed down with the regrets of the past and the reality of the toll that our foolish mistakes have made on the present? Is present day perfection required in order to feel uplifted?

Perfection in this life is our goal, but imperfection or the things of our past should not get us down. We have a glorious future that we strive for. That is our true hope. All other things that we hope for are temporary to this life. We have a greater and lasting hope to fulfill us. We have no need to look back with regret.

Paul could have lived in the depressing despair of regret for all that he had done. He persecuted Christians. He even had them killed. How do you think he lived with himself? He didn't look back; he looked ahead to the life Christ set before him. He lived in the present by the power of Jesus Christ.

Not that I have already attained this—that is, I have not already been perfected—but I strive to lay hold of that for which Christ Jesus also laid hold of me. Brothers and sisters, I do not consider myself to have attained this. Instead I am single-minded: **Forgetting the things that are behind and reaching out for the things that are ahead**, with this goal in mind, I strive toward the prize of the upward call of God in Christ Jesus. Therefore let those of us who are "perfect" embrace this point of view. If you think otherwise, God will reveal to you the error of your ways. Nevertheless, let us live up to the standard that we have already attained. Philippians 3:12-16 (NET)

Jesus came to make it possible to refrain from our destructive life of sin and to pursue a life of righteousness that results in life—eternal life. What encouragement! What hope! This is a real hope, one that plays out in our daily lives. It is the hope to live a different life that is truly life. And it is empowered by God.

Jesus sees the toll that sin has had on our individual lives, and he longs for us to turn from the deathly way of our lives and to turn toward him in order to have his life. He looks at us with love, not with judgment. He is the one who reaches out to us and leads us to repent so that we can truly live. This is our encouragement in the midst of our struggles.

Don't you see how wonderfully kind, tolerant, and patient God is with you? Does this mean nothing to you? Can't you see that his kindness is intended to turn you from your sin? Romans 2:4 (NLT)

Jesus answered them, "Those who are well don't need a physician, but those who are sick do. I have not come to call the righteous, but sinners to repentance." Luke 5:31-32 (NET)

If our depression is fueled by regret over our past, then the deliverance is to focus on the glorious future Jesus provides for us if we will only turn to him in faith and obedience so that we can live a new life from now and into the future. Repentance brings the hope of a new life. If we have dug a deep hole, we will likely have to climb out. But Jesus provides the way out for those who repent. The hope of his abundant life—even while still in our struggles—encourages and delivers from depression. Our sorrowful regrets turn into hope.

For the kind of sorrow God wants us to experience leads us away from sin and results in salvation. There's no regret for that kind of sorrow. But worldly sorrow, which lacks repentance, results in spiritual death. 2 Corinthians 7:10 (NLT)

Now the Lord is the Spirit, and where the Spirit of the Lord is, there is freedom. And we all, with unveiled face, beholding the glory of the Lord, are being transformed into the same image from one degree of glory to another. For this comes from the Lord who is the Spirit. 2 Corinthians 3:17-18 (ESV)

God's Regret and Hope Versus Our Regret and Hope

God's regret is due to our choice to live our lives apart from God where we can make our own choices without God's direction. We have been deceitfully manipulated into believing that God's ways are controlling and that there is more life to be found by going it alone. But our going it alone without a submissive, obedient relationship with God is what gets us into trouble with our lives. *Independence from God is the root cause of making regretful choices in life.*

Think about it. God's regret comes from the same source. It is not that he regrets his perfect plan, but rather, he regrets our rebellion against his perfect plan. From that standpoint he grieves over creating us. The source of our regret is the same as God's regret—man's rebellion against God. If we had all just lived life his way in obedience to his counsel, directions and warnings, we would have prospered in this life without limit. In essence, we robbed ourselves of the blessings of God. There cannot be any greater regret. And this regret is felt by God and man.

But we have a great hope. God has provided a way to redeem his creation so that both God and man will once again live in unity with him for eternity and experience his life flowing in and among us. This is the "good news". All regrets will be a thing of the past and left there. This is our great hope. God and man share in this same hope.

Then I saw a new heaven and a new earth, for the first heaven and the first earth had passed away, and there was no longer any sea. I saw the Holy City, the new Jerusalem, coming down out of heaven from God, **prepared as a bride beautifully dressed for her husband**. And I heard a loud voice from the throne saying, "**Now the dwelling of God is with men, and he will live with them. They will be his people, and God himself will be with them and be their God**. He will wipe every tear from their eyes. There will be no more death or mourning or crying or pain, for **the old order of things has passed away**."

He who was seated on the throne said, "**I am making everything new!**" Then he said, "Write this down, for these words are trustworthy and true."

He said to me: "It is done. I am the Alpha and the Omega, the Beginning and the End. To him who is thirsty I will give to drink without cost from the spring of the water of life. He who overcomes will inherit all this, and **I will be his God and he will be my son**. Revelation 21:1-7 (NIV)

This is our eternal hope. And when this hope is fulfilled, all past regrets will have been redeemed and will lose their power. There will be no depression in God's holy, living and loving presence—only peace and joy. What a glorious future is in store for us whose hope is in Christ.

We wait in hope, but God has given us his own Spirit to sustain us while we wait. He has given us his own Spirit to begin his process of redemption in our heart, mind and soul now while we wait for the glorious appearing of Jesus' return. Then our transformation will be complete and instant—in the blink of an eye. (1 Corinthians 15:52)

Therefore, since we have been declared righteous by faith, we have peace with God through our Lord Jesus Christ, through whom we have also obtained access by faith into this grace in which we stand, and **we rejoice in the hope of God's glory**. Not only this, but we also rejoice in sufferings, knowing that suffering produces endurance, and endurance, character, and character, hope. **And hope does not disappoint, because the love of God has been poured out in our hearts through the Holy Spirit who was given to us**. Romans 5:1-5 (NET)

Blessed be the God and Father of our Lord Jesus Christ! By his great mercy he gave us **new birth into a living hope through the resurrection of Jesus Christ from the dead**, that is, into an inheritance imperishable, undefiled, and unfading. It is reserved in heaven for you, who by God's power are protected through faith for a salvation ready to be revealed in the last time. 1 Peter 1:3-5 (NET)

Reflection Questions

If you could go back in time, what things would you do different?

What mistakes of your past burden you today? Describe your regret and any depression that you feel as a result.

Describe your hope for your future?

Describe your hope in what God is doing in you and in your life. What is your future, eternal hope? How are you making strides toward your eternal hope now? How does that make you feel?

Chapter 12

Frustration and Disappointment

We have already discussed having major setbacks in one's life, and for sure, they can be very frustrating with huge disappointments. Frustrations may be from a long-term setback, but they can be just a series of frustrating daily setbacks. Maybe you begin your day knowing that you have a lot on your plate, or at least you have a lot that you expect to achieve this day. You start by getting on the internet to check your calendar and get caught up on your daily emails. Not a big deal. But as soon as you get started, you find that you don't have a connection, and you don't know why. Maybe the server is down, or maybe it is your modem, or your router. You now take a diversion in your plans, and begin troubleshooting your internet problem. After a half hour and no success, you give up, but the calendar and emails are still in need. Your plate is full, and you don't know how you are going to get everything done in one day. To top it all off, your phone rings and it is your daughter who just called to talk. Now the day is another hour shorter, and you realize that you haven't showered, dressed, ate breakfast, read your Bible and prayed yet. The clock is ticking; you have company coming for dinner, and you don't know what to make, and after you figure that out, you still will have to go out grocery shopping, not to mention clean the house for guests.

This example is a frustrating day, but what if we are experiencing a frustrating life. Suppose you are unemployed. We all have bills to pay and things to buy. We all need to eat and have a place to live. So you have been looking for a job. You have applied to many, but to date, you have had no offers. You are still unemployed with no obvious prospects and no obvious means for supporting yourself and your family. Frustration and disappointment builds—depression sets in.

Frustrations occur when the demands put upon our lives are greater than our ability to meet those demands. Sometimes these demands come from someone else, and sometimes the demands come from our choices and desires. We may have set some unreasonable expectations that we failed to accomplish.

We all face frustrations and disappointments from time to time. Becoming frustrated does not automatically progress into being depressed. But what if our lives feel like one big and continuous frustration and disappointment with no obvious way of escape? Now we are back to losing our hope. No one likes frustration. In fact, *frustration is what happens when we unsuccessfully try to alleviate a situation that is undesirable.* Some of us are more persistent than others, which means we will try harder and longer before getting frustrated. It is like having a larger frustration tolerance. And we would all be better off if we were more patiently persistent when confronted with difficulties. But what if we fail to overcome our difficulties, no matter how long or how hard we work at it? Unresolved frustration can easily lead to depression.

So what is the solution to our depression? There are several possibilities.

One, solve the frustration. But that is not so easy, especially since we may have already spent our energies on a solution.

The second solution is to ask for help. Many life problems can be resolved when we call upon someone to come to our aid. They may have some knowhow that we don't have. Maybe we just need another's perspective on the problem. Maybe just having someone to share the load is all that we needed. Maybe we just needed a friend at our side.

And third, seek God for help. Actually, this should not be third; it should be first. We should be seeking him before we even begin a challenge.

I remember being confronted with a very serious and frustrating problem once when I worked in the chemical industry. I had developed a process with a new technology for a new product form. I had spent a lot of the company's money on this process based on my ingenuity and recommendations. "It had to work!" A stainless steel piston extruder was a critical component. But when a stainless steel piston slides through a stainless steel sleeve with close tolerances, it has a strong tendency to gall. Galling is like welding the two parts together. And that is exactly what I experienced. It took a 100 ton press to separate them.

The company had all sorts of material experts, so I called upon them for advice. I made change after change with various coatings, change of tolerances—whatever the experts suggested. And every time, with every change, it failed. The piston and sleeve galled and froze up solid. I had persevered over many weeks of trying. I had called upon the experts. Nothing worked. I was frustrated, disappointed and very concerned. I had spent a lot of the company's money at my recommendation. They trusted me, and now I was failing them and myself. And my career would suffer the consequences.

I know that I had prayed along the way. I always pray about what is going on in my daily life. But now I was trapped in a corner with no obvious way of escape. I called out to the Lord to help me. That day I was sitting at my desk. On the book shelf immediately in front of me was a forty year old Mechanical Engineer's Handbook. I was moved inside to take a look inside that book and look in the section on bearing materials. And sure enough; it recommended using a brass sleeve for a stainless shaft. And brass was compatible with our product. The problem was solved; the galling ceased. The solution to my problem was sitting in my office all this time, and it was right within my reach. It was hidden in a forty year old handbook. I am still perplexed that the material experts did not suggest this solution. Maybe it was God who kept the solution from me because he was just waiting for me to call upon him in my despair.

Not all of our frustrating circumstances are removed by God. Sometimes the frustration is borne out of our own attitudes. We may be a perfectionist, so when everything is not just the way we want them to be, we become frustrated. For example, maybe you have a heavy schedule where your day is all planned out for each individual expectation. But then the day does not proceed as you planned it. There are interruptions that add to your agenda. There are some things that take longer than you thought. And maybe you needed to buy something and it was out of stock or you couldn't find it. If you are a perfectionist, most days will turn out like this, and you will become frustrated and tense. Your bad attitude will affect your relationships, and now you will have one more burden to carry. Perfectionists are seeking approval and happiness in their perfection, but they are a setup for disappointment and frustration. The root cause is not the out-of-your-control circumstances, but a heart of perfectionism. A life of perfectionism can lead to a life of depression. God is not going to make everything perfect to your every whim or definitions of perfect. But he will change your heart—if you are willing and ask him for the change.

There are times when our frustrating circumstances are orchestrated by God. He may give us peace in the midst of them, but he is not necessarily going to remove them. Think of Moses in the desert for forty years with over a million complaining Israelites. Think of the promise to Abraham to be a father of many nations through his offspring, but his wife Sarah was barren. God finally came through with his promise, but Abraham was one hundred years old and Sarah was ninety. Think of Joseph who was rejected by his brothers, sold as a slave, falsely accused and sent to prison for many years. He was eventually released and became second in command of Egypt, but he had to endure many years of hardship beforehand without knowing what was in his future.

All of these men were called by God to fulfill a portion of history for the purposes of God. He calls us in similar fashion. We are not typically made aware of God's plans. We certainly do not know the detailed circumstances and timings. We just have to endure in faith and trust in God for his honor and glory to be revealed in our lives, for his will to be done. And that is the key. We usually are seeking God to answer our prayers in order to fulfill our will, not God's will. Suffering is not our will. Who wants to suffer? *Frustration comes out of suffering without deliverance, but expecting deliverance. Frustration comes out of attempting to control the details of our lives, but failing in our attempts.*

God calls us to persevere, to overcome, to endure. If all of our circumstances were pleasant, there would be no need to persevere, overcome or endure. So many times in our life, the answer is not for our life to change, but for our view of our life to change. And when our view changes, so will our attitude. And if our frustrations are depressing, the answer to our depression is to have God's perspective and God's attitude toward our life circumstances.

I know men in prison with life sentences. Some are clearly guilty, but their lives have totally changed because they have become Christians and he has changed who they are now. But that does not change their life prison sentence. Some claim that they were falsely accused, and that may be true, but their prison sentence may never change. How does one maintain joy when subjected to such disappointment and such confinement? It all comes down to trusting God and living for him in the midst of our unwanted circumstances. Frustration and disappointment does not bring about the glory of God, but it can rob us of joy and replace it with depression.

I know of many women who have divorced their husbands because they had different expectations of what their marriage would bring to them. I am not even referring to abusive husbands; just regular responsible guys. But these wives claim that they put up with the frustration of their husbands for too long. They claim that God wants them to be happy, and their husbands are robbing them of happiness. So they leave and file for divorce. As I look at their lives years later, I don't see any great blessings of happiness. They made a choice to run from their marriage out of frustration that was based in selfishness. God is not going to deliver us from life circumstances because we are not thankful and appreciative of what he has provided for us. But he may deliver us from being selfish. Self-focused people struggle with frustration and depression. Self-sacrificing people who give out of a true love for God and others find peace and joy and a rich blessing from God in their lives.

Carrying One Another's Burdens

We live in an isolated society. For the most part it is a world of every man and woman striving for their own security and happiness by themselves without others to come alongside of them. Very few look out for their neighbor. As a consequence, when frustrating circumstances arise, we are faced to struggle alone. In fact, if we were not alone in our struggles, frustrations may not even occur.

God created mankind to live out our lives in communal harmony with one another. God created man to rule over and do the work of maintaining his earthly creation. God assessed everything that he made and said that it was good. That is, except one thing. He said that it was not good for man to be alone. So he created for him a helpmate or companion. He made a woman out of the flesh of the man. Now they were two separate people made from one, but then he married them and said that they were now one (again). Now the man did not have to work alone; he had a helpmate, a compatible companion to work with. (Genesis 2:15-25) Working alone can be lonely and frustrating; whereas working together can be joyful and satisfying.

Solomon wrote about the strength of working together with a partner in life's work.

Two people are better than one, because they can reap more benefit from their labor. For if they fall, one will help his companion up, but pity the person who falls down and has no one to help him up. Furthermore, if two lie down together, they can keep each other warm, but how can one person keep warm by himself? Although an assailant may overpower one person, two can withstand him. Moreover, a three-stranded cord is not quickly broken. Ecclesiastes 4:9-12 (NET)

We were created to live our lives in cooperation and unity with others. Furthermore, notice that Solomon's statement begins with two people, but ends with a three stranded cord. I suggest that God is the third strand. There is no place for frustration and dependence when we have a partner in life, and together you invite God into the relationship. "For nothing is impossible with God." (Luke 1:37) That is a "three-stranded cord that is not quickly broken".

Frustration is typically the result of carrying our own burdens with no one to call upon. Marriage has been given to us by God for this very purpose, to have a partner in life. Part of God's work was for man to populate the earth, so he created marriage and family. Not all marriages are good partnerships, but that is because of our sin. Remember, Adam and Eve were perfectly united before they chose to live life independent of God. That is when they realized their nakedness and hid from each other and from God. We have been suffering the separations ever since. But that does not change our need for working in unity with each other, and with God, obediently under his directives and his provision.

Life is filled with many burdens. One of God's curses upon man for his choice to disobey was that he would make his work toilsome. In addition, we have all become disobedient sinners, living out life apart from God's ways of living for a prosperous true life. We have all reaped the frustrations of our own sin, for sin robs us of life. We are instructed to come alongside of each other in our frustrating struggle against sin. Even in this struggle, we need one another.

> Brothers and sisters, if a person is discovered in some sin, you who are spiritual restore such a person in a spirit of gentleness. Pay close attention to yourselves, so that you are not tempted too. Carry one another's burdens, and in this way you will fulfill the law of Christ. Galatians 6:1-2 (NET)

This is a twofold responsibility. We are created to live in unity with one another. Whether we are the one walking in sin or the one who comes alongside the one who struggles, we both have the same responsibility to seek each other out.

Is anyone among you suffering? He should pray. Is anyone in good spirits? He should sing praises. Is anyone among you ill? **He should summon the elders of the church**, and they should pray for him and anoint him with oil in the name of the Lord. And the prayer of faith will save the one who is sick and the Lord will raise him up—and if he has committed sins, he will be forgiven. **So confess your sins to one another and pray for one another so that you may be healed**. The prayer of a righteous person has great effectiveness. James 5:13-16 (NET)

Certainly, life is filled with disappointments, setbacks, suffering and hardships. Just having others at your side does not mean that nothing will be hard, painful or disappointing. But it does mean that we can survive the struggles of life with victory. We were created by God to have intimate fellowship with one another. This means that we live together with nothing to hide. Remember, Adam and Eve covered themselves with fig leaves to hide from each other. Before they disobeyed God they were naked and without shame. As long as we continue to hide from each other, not making ourselves vulnerable, we will not experience the power and support of being united with others. And, when we come together in openness to each other, we are also inviting God into our midst. Remember, Adam and Eve hid from each other, but then they hid from God. If we are to have true fellowship with one another and with God, we have to come out of hiding. This is the true understanding of walking in the light. It is not that we hide our sin, weaknesses, flaws, mistakes or failures, but that we expose them under the loving eyes of our brothers and sisters of Christ and before God.

This is the message we heard from Jesus and now declare to you: God is light, and there is no darkness in him at all. So we are lying if we say we have fellowship with God but go on living in spiritual darkness; we are not practicing the truth. But if we are living in the light, as God

189

is in the light, then we have fellowship with each other, and the blood of Jesus, his Son, cleanses us from all sin.

If we claim we have no sin, we are only fooling ourselves and not living in the truth. But **if we confess our sins to him**, he is faithful and just to forgive us our sins and to cleanse us from all wickedness. If we claim we have not sinned, we are calling God a liar and showing that his word has no place in our hearts. 1 John 1:5-10 (NLT)

Jesus Sought Out the Help of Others

Jesus is fully God, and as he walked on this earth, he was also fully human. He was like you and me with all of our earthly needs. He became hungry, he slept, he had to walk from place to place—and he felt physical and emotional pain. Many people, in addition to his disciples, served his physical needs.

Jesus was God, but he was also man with all of man's pains, enemies and weaknesses. Jesus faced his greatest attack and pain in the last days of his life. In the garden he prayed, and he asked his closest disciples to pray with him. (Mark 14:32-42) In his greatest torment, he called out to God, and God sent angels to strengthen him. (Luke 22:39-46) After being beaten and mocked, he was commanded to carry a heavy cross to his crucifixion. It was too heavy, and someone helped him carry his cross. (Matthew 27:32) Jesus was God, but as a man, he had all of our human weaknesses. And as such, he called out for and depended upon the help of others. That is how God created us. We need one another.

Entering God's Rest for Our Souls

Isolating the real man inside from others and from God only makes us weak. And then we become a victim of life's difficulties and succumb to frustration, loneliness and depression. True rest for our souls is derived from a truthful relationship with our heavenly Father and Jesus through his body. But most of us do not know how to rest. Rest ultimately comes from

God who invites us into his rest. That is what the Sabbath rest signifies. We are all invited to rest in God's rest, but we don't know how. We were born into a world that thrives on hiding and independence from God. We feel as though we have to make it through life on our own in our own strength. But what happens when we are not enough to make it through the difficult journey of life? The burdens become too much for us. Jesus invites us to call out to him so that he can teach us to rest.

> Come to me, all you who are weary and burdened, and I will give you rest. Take my yoke on you and learn from me, because I am gentle and humble in heart, and **you will find rest for your souls**. For my yoke is easy to bear, and my load is not hard to carry." Matthew 11:28-30 (NET)

A yoke is a wooden device that allows two oxen to pull a plow together. They both work alongside of each other to plow the same field. Notice that there are two actions to Jesus' invitation. Jesus invites us to take his yoke. That means that we have to get rid of our yoke. Jesus is not saying that he will come into our field and help us plow by taking up our yoke. He is saying that we have to leave our yoke and our field. Then we are to come over into his field and plow together with him. So we discard our yoke and take up his.

What might this look like? Let's use money for an example. It is not wrong to have money or to use it. But it is wrong to make a god out of it. Jesus said that we cannot depend on both. We can choose to rest in our money based on our own strength and provision or to rest in God for our strength and provision.

"No one can serve two masters, for either he will hate the one and love the other, or he will be devoted to the one and despise the other. You cannot serve God and money.

"Therefore I tell you, do not worry about your life, what you will eat or drink, or about your body, what you will wear. Isn't there more to life than food and more to the body than clothing? Look at the birds in the sky: They do not sow, or reap, or gather into barns, yet your heavenly Father feeds them. Aren't you more valuable than they are? And which of you by worrying can add even one hour to his life? Why do you worry about clothing? Think about how the flowers of the field grow; they do not work or spin. Yet I tell you that not even Solomon in all his glory was clothed like one of these! And if this is how God clothes the wild grass, which is here today and tomorrow is tossed into the fire to heat the oven, won't he clothe you even more, you people of little faith? So then, don't worry saying, 'What will we eat?' or 'What will we drink?' or 'What will we wear?' For the unconverted pursue these things, and your heavenly Father knows that you need them. **But above all pursue his kingdom and righteousness, and all these things will be given to you as well**. So then, do not worry about tomorrow, for tomorrow will worry about itself. Today has enough trouble of its own. Matthew 6:24-34 (NET)

To come into God's rest requires of us to make a choice. What choice are we making regarding money? Does this mean that we can no longer have money or use money? No, but it does mean that we can no longer love money. We can no longer look to money as our security, worth and source of happiness. God is our security, our worth and our source of joy. We can still use money; the real question is "where is the love of our heart?" What is our heart's desire? If it is money, we will love money. If it is God, we will love God.

Delight yourself in the LORD, and he will give you the desires of your heart. Commit your way to the LORD; trust in him, and he will act. He will bring forth your righteousness as the light, and your justice as the noonday. Psalm 37:4-6 (ESV)

Jesus says that we are to pursue his kingdom and righteousness, and then God would give us all the things and money that we need. (Matthew

6:33) God does not have a problem with riches and possessions as long as we do not have them at a higher priority in our heart than we do the things of God, namely his kingdom and righteousness. Where is our heart? That is the real question. Are we resting in God, or in our own strength?

We have used money to illustrate resting in God rather than in our own capability. And money is a major concern in this regard. But there are other dependencies that will rob us of joy and peace. We may seek our careers and the status and recognition they provide. We may seek beauty and popularity. We may seek achievements, especially if they are competitive in nature with the ability to raise ourselves up in comparison to others. We may seek recreational pursuits, such as sports, travel, hobbies. None of these are wrong, but, again, we have to be aware of why they have become so important. Have we replaced God with gods of our own making for happiness? They will eventually let us down, and then what will we have?

Our own strength will fail us. And when we realize that we have failed, we can fall victim to frustration, disappointment, fear and anxiety, culminating in depression. The antidote is rest in God.

Caution: We don't seek rest because we are now depressed. We seek rest because we love God and put our faith in him. Joy and peace are the outcomes. Seeking rest with the wrong motive may not result in true rest.

Reflection Questions

Are you frequently frustrated or disappointed with your life? What frustrates you most?

What frustrations in your life could have been circumvented if you had lived differently? How does that make you feel?

What frustrations are out of your control and were not a consequence of your own decisions or behaviors? How are you struggling to accept these life situations as God's will for you?

Who do you have in this life to come alongside of you in the midst of life's burdens?

Do you come alongside of others when they are struggling? Give some examples of whom and how you supported them in their struggles.

How are you resting in God? How are you seeking other things of this life for security and identity rather than God?

Chapter 13

Unfulfilled Hopes

Hope is opposite to depression. Our lives can be filled with hardships and struggles, but we can move forward because we have hope for the future. On the other hand, without hope, even if we are not experiencing pain in our lives, just the absence of hope can drag us down into depression. God created our lives to have purpose. We look to the future to see where we are going, what we are becoming, what we will be doing, how our lives will prosper. God created us to live in hope. A lack of hope can make us sick inside.

> Hope deferred makes the heart sick, but a longing fulfilled is like a tree of life. Proverbs 13:12 (NET)

How far ahead do we hope? If I have good things in store for today, but tomorrow's hopes are empty, will I be joyfully hopeful? Not likely. Hope is in the future. It is a confident understanding that today may be a struggle or disappointment, but that will all change for the better a ways down the road of my life.

For example, you may struggle to go to college. It requires large amounts of money and many long hours of study—days and years of study. But you are driven and encouraged because of the hope of someday having a good career that will bring lasting enjoyment and purpose. It will also provide all the finances needed for you and your family. This is an example of investing in your skill development for four to eight years in order to secure a career that will last thirty to fifty years. The relatively short hardships are worth the lifelong reward.

Another example might be saving up a portion of every paycheck so that you can buy a house in ten years. You save in the hope of living in your own home. The hope drives you and encourages you to save.

Life Requires Hope

Our lives are filled with hopeful endeavors. But what happens if we do not have any hopes? Hope is a lifeline. The proverb above says that "a longing fulfilled is like a tree of life". That is a very powerful truth. We die inside without hope. There are only eleven occurrences of the tree of life in the entire Bible. Three of these are in the early part of Genesis. Remember that the tree of life was in the Garden of Eden, but when man rebelled against God, we all lost direct access to this life-giving tree which would provide the nourishment to live forever. Four of these references to the tree of life are in the Revelation to John, where we read about how we gain back our access to the tree of life through Jesus. And there are four references in Proverbs that lend a certain understanding of the fruit of this tree.

- Wisdom (Proverbs 3:18)
- Fruit of righteousness (Proverbs 11:30)
- **Fulfilled hope**, a longing fulfilled (Proverbs 13:12)
- Gentle speech that heals the soul (Proverbs 15:4)

Hope is included in this short list of attributes for the tree of life. Having a hope fulfilled is a tree of life. It should be obvious that hope is an essential component for true life. Hope sustains us through hardships, pain, disappointments and painful struggles of most any kind.

Ultimate Hope

We can hope for today. We can hope for tomorrow, next week, next year or ten years from now. So what is the ultimate hope? Our ultimate hope is when this life, as we know it, is over and, for those who are in Christ Jesus, we obtain the glorious freedom of the children of God. Notice in the follow passage how often hope is described as a future expectation.

> Yet what we suffer now is nothing compared to the glory he will reveal to us later. For **all creation is waiting eagerly for that future day** when God will reveal who his children really are. Against its will, all creation was subjected to God's curse. But **with eager hope, the creation looks forward to the day when** it will join God's children in glorious freedom from death and decay. For we know that all creation has been groaning as in the pains of childbirth right up to the present time. And we believers also groan, even though we have the Holy Spirit within us as a **foretaste of future glory**, for we **long for** our bodies to be released from sin and suffering. We, too, **wait with eager hope for the day when** God will give us our full rights as his adopted children, including the new bodies he has promised us. We were given this hope when we were saved. (**If we already have something, we don't need to hope for it. But if we look forward to something we don't yet have, we must wait patiently and confidently**.) Romans 8:18-25 (NLT)

Hope sustains us. Hope is a focus on a future that has the promise of good things for our lives. Some hope comes without effort, but that is usually when the future we hope for is only a short time away, like tomorrow or next week or even next month. It is like anticipating a vacation that is only a few months away. But what happens if we are in the midst of what seems like endless struggles with no hope of escape in sight? What if there is hope, but it is a long time away—maybe many years? Now the hope is not automatic; we have to choose to focus on our distant hope.

197

Jesus suffered the cross for the joy set before him. (Hebrews 12:2) Jesus knows what it means to focus on future glory in the midst of immense suffering. Many times we are called to do the same.

What if your life is filled with failure? What if you are addicted to drugs or alcohol? What if you struggled for years to escape the bondage, but you have not succeeded. Now you have no hope. You started your addiction because you felt hopeless, and now the devastation brought on by having no hope of becoming sober only makes you more depressed.

What if your spouse died or divorced you? What hope is there to get her back? Or maybe you have been convicted of a crime and now you are in prison with a long sentence. What hope do you have now? Any dreams that you had or were pursuing have lost all hope in being fulfilled.

A loss of hope can devastate us! It is critically imperative to persevere in our hope. It takes a committed determination to focus on and strive for our future goal with the hopeful expectation of reaching it. And the only concrete future goal that will take us into eternity is the goal of being transformed into the likeness of Jesus Christ, to be delivered from our sinful nature, to cross over from this world of sin that is ruled by the devil and to enter the glorious kingdom of God with Jesus as King and Lord. That is a hopeful goal that will sustain us if we keep faith, strive to obtain it without looking back and then to persevere till the end. That is how Paul led his life in the midst of endless hardships.

> **Not that I have already reached [the goal]** or am already fully mature, but I make every effort to take hold of it because I also have been taken hold of by Christ Jesus. Brothers, I do not consider myself to have taken hold of it. But one thing I do: **Forgetting what is behind and reaching forward to what is ahead, I pursue as my goal** the prize promised by God's heavenly call in Christ Jesus. Therefore, **all who are mature should think this way.** Philippians 3:12-15 (HCSB)

We have a glorious hope, but it may not find its fulfillment for many more earthly years. Some of us lose patience and endurance. Some of us are distracted by a hope that is much sooner and more readily available. But one thing is for sure; we will all die. Then there is only one hope that counts. It is a hope that carries into eternity. Paul wrote about this hope, and he comments on the futility of those whose hope is merely short-term.

> If only for this life we have hope in Christ, we are to be pitied more than all men. 1 Corinthians 15:19 (NIV)

The Hope of God's Strength in Our Troubles

We have another hope in the meantime while we struggle in this life; God will come to our aid in the midst of our struggles if we will call out to him. We are forever dependent upon him for all things. There is no security in life other than God. There is no life apart from God, for God is life—he defines true life. We are completely dependent upon him for whatever good things we hope for. So in our distress, what else can we do other than call out to him for mercy?

> Be merciful to me, O LORD, for I am in distress; my eyes grow weak with sorrow, my soul and my body with grief. My life is consumed by anguish and my years by groaning; my strength fails because of my affliction, and my bones grow weak. Psalm 31:9-10 (NIV)

We could quote hundreds of verses in this regard. Let's consider a few of them. Man was created to have sustaining life by remaining connected with God. This connection has several aspects, but it must be understood that we were created to be totally dependent upon God for everything. Man attempted to separate himself from God and to go out into life apart from God. This is the essence of Adam and Eve eating from the tree that God warned them not to eat or they would die. It was a tree that held within it the thought of being wise enough to live on our own, not needing God. Man was created to live forever, but God warned them that if they ate of the tree of the knowledge of good and evil that they would die. The devil told them that God had lied to them because he knew that if they did eat of it, they would be like God. They chose to believe the devil rather than God and ate of the forbidden tree. They disobeyed, and death entered in.

We are not totally separated from God. God is still very much a part of his creation. If not, we wouldn't even have one breath of life. We lost access to the paradise of the Garden of Eden, but God has not abandoned mankind. In fact he has always been very much a part of our lives, in spite of our rebellious and sinful behavior. He even cancelled our debt of sin against him and sent his own Spirit to live within us who have repented and believe in Jesus so that we might be reunited.

The hardships, disappointments, suffering and despair of this life are because we chose to become separate from God. But God has made a way for us to return to him and to have the relationship he intended from the beginning. This is our hope as we struggle through this life. Yes, we have a hope of someday experiencing a completely restored relationship with God in the paradise of his kingdom forever. But as long as we live in these fleshly bodies in this earthly existence, we will still have to struggle. Sin is disobedience to God's ways for us, and we live in a world that is filled with sin and unbelief. The world still refuses to acknowledge God and our need to live according to his ways. But we have a great hope while we live out our days on earth. This hope is founded in the present love of God for those who call out to him. God is very present in the present. He desires to walk along with us in our struggles to show us the way of everlasting so that we can walk in it now.

No one whose **hope is in you** will ever be put to shame, but they will be put to shame who are treacherous without excuse. Show me your ways, O LORD, teach me your paths; guide me in your truth and teach me, for you are God my Savior, and **my hope is in you** all day long. Psalm 25:3-5 (NIV)

This life can be a huge burden to carry. We weren't designed to live life apart from God. We are like little children who run away from home. I have had my own children run away from home when they were just little kids. They wouldn't be gone very long—an hour at most, and they would return. They wanted freedom from authority, but they soon realized that they couldn't survive without Dad and Mom to care for and protect them.

As adult children of God, we would be wise to realize the same thing, that we cannot survive without God. We need him. He is our true refuge from the trials of life. Our soul finds rest in him, and him alone.

Find rest, O my soul, in God alone; **my hope comes from him**. He alone is my rock and my salvation; he is my fortress, I will not be shaken. My salvation and my honor depend on God; he is my mighty rock, my refuge. Trust in him at all times, O people; pour out your hearts to him, for God is our refuge. Psalm 62:5-8 (NIV)

Our waywardness has led us into a loss of true life and into many struggles. But God has given us his word to make us wise and to lead us down his paths of life again. There is great hope in God's word for our lives today.

I desperately long for your deliverance. **I find hope in your word**. My eyes grow tired as I wait for your promise to be fulfilled. I say, "When will you comfort me?" For I am like a wineskin dried up in smoke. I do not forget your statutes. How long must your servant endure this? Psalm 119:81-84 (NET)

I cried out with all my heart, "Answer me, O LORD! I will observe your statutes." I cried out to you, "Deliver me, so that I can keep your rules." I am up before dawn crying for help. **I find hope in your word**. My eyes anticipate the nighttime hours, so that I can meditate on your word. Listen to me because of your loyal love! O LORD, revive me, as you typically do! Those who are eager to do wrong draw near; they are far from your law. You are near, O LORD, and all your commands are reliable. I learned long ago that you ordained your rules to last. Psalm 119:145-152 (NET)

This life is a journey. Each of us has been given a finite number of years. We have a choice to live these years apart from God or in cooperation with God. The choice is ours, but the consequences are God's. One leads to life, and the other to death. It is a choice everyone must make.

As was stated earlier, we live on hope. Man is the only creature of God's creation that looks out into the future. He is the only one who plans for tomorrow—next week—next year—and even decades out into our future lives. God created us this way. We live on hope, and we are all striving to have a hope that will sustain us. But where does a sustaining hope come from? And what is that sustaining hope? Hope is futuristic. "Who hopes for what he already has?" (Romans 8:24)

We have the ability to create all kinds of hopes that never happen because they are not based on God who defines our true hope. Depression comes when we have lost all hope, when our own hopes and dreams fail us, because they are based on our own ability to control the present and the future. But only God has that power. We are totally dependent upon God for true hope. We find rest for our souls when we put our trust and hope in what God has for our lives. We trust him because he is faithful, he is all powerful and because he loves his own children.

How great is the love the Father has lavished on us, that we should be called children of God! And that is what we are! The reason the world does not know us is that it did not know him. Dear friends, now we are children of God, and what we will be has not yet been made known. But **we know that when he appears, we shall be like him,** for we shall see him as he is. **Everyone who has this hope in him purifies himself,** just as he is pure. 1 John 3:1-3 (NIV)

Unfulfilled Hopes

We all want to be in control of our future, but real hope is a hope in God for all things. We do not have the ability to control the outcomes of life. But all things are possible with God, and he is in control of all things. Our true hope is in him, and him alone.

Reflection Questions

What unfulfilled hopes and dreams for this earthly life do you have?

How have your unfulfilled hopes discouraged you?

We all have an earthly life that lasts eighty to ninety years for most of us. And we all will die and pass on to another existence some day. What is your hope for eternity? I am sure you can describe life today; describe the details of the life you hope for.

"For I consider that our present sufferings cannot even be compared to the glory that will be revealed to us." Romans 8:18 (NET) What are your "present sufferings" and how does your hope in "the glory that will be revealed to us" carry you through your struggles? In other words, how does your hope in the next life encourage you in the struggles and disappointments of this life?

Describe your relationship with God. How is God your hope, and how does your relationship with him carry you through your hardships, discouragements and disappointments?

Hope is in the future. God makes many promises in his word. Promises are for the future. What promises of God do you cling to for hope today?

God's word is transforming. It changes our thinking, attitudes and behaviors. In time, these changes in us will bring about a better life. Describe how God's word is changing you and how you are encouraged by the changes regarding who you are as a person. How are these changes blessing your life? How do they increase your hope for your future life?

Chapter 14

The Pain of Loneliness

In the beginning, God created a multitude of living creatures, but only man was created in the image of God. As God progressed on his creation, he declared at the end of each day that his creation was good. But when he created man, he was alone without a mate, and he declared that this was not good.

> The LORD God said, "**It is not good for the man to be alone**. I will make a companion for him who corresponds to him." Genesis 2:18 (NET)

God created all of the various creatures that live upon the earth. Some are social creatures; some are not. Turtles, for instance, are not raised by their parents. The mother turtle lays her eggs in the sand and then goes back out to sea. The new little turtles hatch on their own and go out to sea by themselves, and may never meet their mother or father. They live mostly alone, without communal interactions with other turtles. There is no indication that they need each other or become lonely.

That is not how God created man. God is a relational being. He created man in his own image, so we are relational beings. It is our God-given nature to need one another. When God created a woman out of the man, he was not just creating a mate for man. He was fulfilling the need for relationships, one to another. Marriage is the closest relationship of all relationships. It was created to be lasting, intimate and full of love. From this marriage union come children and family. We were created with a heartfelt need to be part of a family. It is not good for man to be alone. So

God has provided a means to fill our need to be relationally connected to each other. God's heart goes out to those who are lonely, especially those who are alone in this life without a family.

God sets the lonely in families, Psalm 68:6 (NIV)

Loneliness is one of mankind's greatest struggles and pains. We need each other, but we all struggle with loneliness to some degree and at some time. Extended loneliness is like a deep dungeon with no apparent escape. It is life consuming. Loneliness is a very painful, depressing existence. It has the power to cripple all other aspects of our lives. Meaningful, caring, accepting and committed relationships are a basic life need that we all have, but we all struggle to have them.

Loneliness Is Part of the Fall of Mankind

As God said, "It is not good for man to be alone." Loneliness was not part of his originally perfect creation. There was no loneliness before Adam and Eve disobeyed God's warning not to eat of the tree of the knowledge of good and evil. Adam and Eve were naked before one another in body, soul and spirit. They also walked with God daily. There was no cause for loneliness. Relationships were perfect, so every relational need was fulfilled by one another. But that all ended immediately after eating of the forbidden tree. Separation occurred—the birth of loneliness.

Loneliness is one of mankind's most severe pains. Loneliness was not part of God's original creation. Adam and Eve were warned that they should not eat of the forbidden fruit of the tree of the knowledge of good and evil. If they did, they would die. But they did eat, and one aspect of the death that God warned against is loneliness. Loneliness is the pain that we experience when we are separated from one another and from God.

Before eating of the forbidden tree, they were naked before each other. There was no fear of what the other might see. In fact, their intimacy was based on being completely transparent to one another in body, soul and spirit. They trusted each other completely. They were perfectly united. But as soon as they disobeyed God, shame rushed in. They first hid from each other by covering up their nakedness. They were no longer intimate without barriers. Their love for one another was now limited and conditional. They also tried to hide from God. Their once open and trusting relationship with God also lost its intimacy. They still had each other, and they still had God, but not like before. From this point on they had to go through life partly separated from each other and from God. This is why we struggle and suffer from loneliness. It was not God's original intent for us.

Loneliness finds its source from many situations. I remember being lonely as a teenager. We had moved out into a country neighborhood. There were not very many neighbors yet. My parents were usually home, but they spent little time with us children. I had two younger sisters, whom I did not relate to at the time. And I had an older brother whom I looked up to. He was my companion. But when he turned sixteen and could drive, he was always gone having fun with his friends. I remember sitting on the front porch in the summer evenings, wishing that I could be with him and his friends. I was all alone. I could sit on this porch for hours and not see a soul. I felt so isolated, and the pain of loneliness hurt so badly.

At least I had a family. And at least my parents were home every evening. My mother did not work, so she was home for us throughout our growing up years.

Most teens do not have this today. Their parents are divorced, or maybe they never married. And if a child has both parents, it is likely that they both work. Meals together as a family are rare today. Home is really just a house where everyone keeps their things and a place to sleep and shower. Everyone has their own life apart from one another. The home should be a place of safety, togetherness, security, love, comfort and acceptance, but that is not the norm today. It gets worse; today's homes are frequently a place of anger, abuse and discord. So instead of finding a loving place to retreat from the world, children find a home filled with fear and pain.

Where does a teenager go if he cannot seek out his own family for his basic need for intimate connections with others? It is no wonder that teens struggle with depression. It is no wonder that we have teens escaping into drugs, alcohol, self-destruction, gangs, video games and sex. Suicide is a major source of death among teenagers.

Suicide (i.e., taking one's own life) is a serious public health problem that affects even young people. For youth between the ages of 10 and 24, suicide is the third leading cause of death. It results in approximately 4,600 lives lost each year. The top three methods used in suicides of young people include firearm (45%), suffocation (40%), and poisoning (8%).

Deaths from youth suicide are only part of the problem. More young people survive suicide attempts than actually die. A nationwide survey of youth in grades 9–12 in public and private schools in the United States (U.S.) found that 16% of students reported seriously considering suicide, 13% reported creating a plan, and 8% reporting trying to take their own life in the 12 months preceding the survey. Each year, approximately 157,000 youth between the ages of 10 and 24 receive medical care for self-inflicted injuries at Emergency Departments across the U.S.[7]

My struggle with loneliness did not end with my teen years. In my early twenties, I moved away from home and took a job in a new community. I shared an apartment with a fellow college graduate. Making friends and being involved and invited into activities with others was a continual pursuit, like it is with most single adults. But then two things happened that left me alone and stranded. My roommate married and moved out. And, I lost my driver's license for a year. The struggle and pain were nearly

---

[7] "Suicide Prevention." *Centers for Disease Control and Prevention*. Centers for Disease Control and Prevention, 10 Mar. 2015. Web. 23 July 2015. <http://www.cdc.gov/violenceprevention/pub/youth_suicide.html>.

overwhelming. I managed to get through this period. In fact, near the end of this year, I met my lifelong marriage partner. At this writing, we have been married for forty-three years. And over those years we had nine children. Our house was filled with togetherness. Home was not a lonely place. I thank God! But I still remember loneliness, and I do not want to ever return to it.

There were times when my job required of me to travel to Europe. I would be gone for a week or two at a time. I was separated from my loved ones by about five thousand miles, which was mostly ocean. I could not just drive home, even if I wanted. And to make it worse, I was in a country that spoke a foreign language and had a different culture. And they had families of their own. I was separated and alone. And the pain was excruciating. Loneliness is crushing and it can drain the life from our soul.

Loneliness is all about us. I see it among my friends and in the many situations they find themselves. I have friends who are divorced. They go home to an empty house. As a young person, we have the hope of marrying and starting a family. But divorce is the failure to successfully make this happen. And remarriage does not automatically solve our problem. The divorce rate among the previously divorced is higher than for first marriages. I see divorced men and women in their forties, fifties and sixties struggling to replace the intimacy of a family with other types of relationships. But it becomes a continual daily struggle that is never satisfied.

Years ago when our children were small, as a family, we visited a county home for people who cannot live independently. Some of these people were destitute and without family. Some had nearby family, and got regular visits, but most of their hours and days were spent without them. They lived in a public residence where they had to find comfort among others with similar struggles of loneliness. And many had nearby family members who did not visit. How terrible to be among people, but feel alone.

I see people in the mall who are not there to shop. They are not there to walk for exercise. They are there to escape loneliness by being among a mall full of strangers. They come and do not actually talk with or relate to anyone. They just come to be around people. It is better than being all alone at home.

I have been involved in prison ministries for many years. I have many close friends in prison. I see firsthand the struggles they carry by being separated and many times rejected by their loved ones—wife, children, parents, relatives, church and old friends. And they feel rejected by society for being a felon in prison. These are fellow human beings who have the same basic needs of all mankind. The most essential of these needs is to be connected with others—a need to love and be loved. And they cannot even take a walk at the mall. They have no opportunity to form the normal relationships that we all take for granted. They cannot ask someone to go out to dinner and have a pleasant conversation and enjoy a part of life together. They cannot play with their children, help them with their homework, go to sport activities, go places together or just hold them and enjoy their presence. Freedom has been denied, and their ability to connect with others in normal social settings is out of reach. Trapped in confinement, depression is always knocking at their door. That is why Jesus said that to love him included visiting those in prison. (Matthew 25:36) Lonely people are all around us. We have an obligation to visit the lonely.

I am sixty-eight at the time of this writing. Statistically, my average life expectancy is about eighty-five. That is only seventeen years away. I see many others who have lost their spouse and are left all alone. And as men and women age, they begin to lose their capacity to do the things that they took for granted just a few years earlier. They may become housebound. They may lose their driver's license, so they cannot shop or visit. They may lose part of their mental capacities and physical capabilities. And all of these losses contribute to confinement and loneliness. They suffer at the end of their lives, and much of the time they suffer alone.

We have churches across this nation. Most meet every Sunday morning. But churches can be very lonely places. Church services are not designed for intimate relationships. The setting is arranged like a theater where the spectators focus on the stage. Talking is seen as a distraction to others who are focused on what is being presented. At the beginning there may be a "meet-and-greet" for two minutes where everyone shakes hands, smiles and says they are fine. But many of those hands are connected to someone struggling with loneliness, although people's inner struggles are not exposed. For the most part, we come as strangers and leave as strangers. We can come lonely and leave lonely.

This is not just a mega-church scenario. I have seen this social atmosphere even in small churches of a hundred to two hundred. People tend to gather in small circles of close friends. The stranger is overlooked. Because they are overlooked, they do not stay to linger during more social times. And, I suppose, many do not come back.

We know that teenagers form natural groups of clicks. Everyone struggles to be accepted. Adults do the same thing. We are naturally drawn to others with a common bond. It could be children, work, hobbies, recreational activities, social status or whatever identity tends to draw us together. The lonely enter our midst, but many are not invited to enter our selective circles. If you are one of these, you know how it feels to be left out. It is a lonely place.

I love to walk. I walk neighborhoods wherever I go. When I was a kid, going for a walk was a social activity. Others were out walking. People were out in their yards. But that has changed. Today most people stay cooped up in their house. They spend time on a number of electronic devices. When they do decide to come out, the automatic garage door opens. They get in the car and drive off, as they close the garage door again with a button. Neighbors hardly know one another anymore. Neighborhoods can be very lonely places.

Apartment buildings are no different. Here people live wall-to-wall from each other, and everyone is a stranger. We live in a very lonely world.

Loneliness is one of the most painful feelings of depression. Loneliness is the feeling of being deprived of our most basic spiritual need—loving, intimate relationships with others. Loneliness is a pandemic!

Escaping Loneliness

Now what do we do? How do we overcome the depression of loneliness?

We would all like the solution for our loneliness to be a loving home with husband, wife, mom, dad, brothers and sisters, but this ideal is not always possible. For many, it is impossible, or at best, very distant. The Scriptures tell the truth.

> Hope deferred makes the heart sick, but a longing fulfilled is like a tree of life. Proverbs 13:12 (NET)

If our heart's focus remains on the hope of something that is far from our reach, it is likely that we will make our heart sick in our endless and disappointing strivings. The cure for our sick heart is to strive for something that is within our reach. Jesus gave us a simple command, to love each other, and in so doing, we will overflow with joy.

> When you obey my commandments, you remain in my love, just as I obey my Father's commandments and remain in his love. **I have told you these things so that you will be filled with my joy. Yes, your joy will overflow! This is my commandment: Love each other in the same way I have loved you.** There is no greater love than to lay down one's life for one's friends. John 15:10-13 (NLT)

We are not in control of other people's love for us, but we can chose to love other people. Loneliness is widespread. We are all exposed to people who struggle with loneliness. What a pathetic irony; lonely people live next door to each other. They walk the same mall at the same time. They go to the same church and live in the same community. If they had each other in their lives, they wouldn't be so lonely. But in their isolation, loneliness overwhelms them. So how does one break free from this dungeon of depressing loneliness?

We can reach out to others who are lonely. Loving others is one escape from being lonely. Everyone struggles with their need for others. Instead of waiting for someone to enter your life, be the one to enter their life. Prisoners are lonely, so visit them. I have been part of prisoner's lives for decades, and I have never been so appreciated. The elderly are lonely, so visit them. They may live in your neighborhood, so knock on their door and introduce yourself. Invite them into your home. Your home is likely one of your most lonely places, so fill it with people. Single people (divorced, widowed, never married) are lonely, so invite them over. Include them in your activities. Make them part of your family.

When I first came to the Lord, I volunteered for an organization that helped needy people with home repairs. I did this for a few years, but as we added children to our growing family, I felt that I needed to change my priorities to my family. I knew that God called us to love one another, and that was what I was doing. So now I was torn about how to reach out and be with my family too. One morning I poured out my dilemma to God, and then got in my car and drove to work. On the way, God spoke to me. He said, "Go to Pinecrest Home; you can take your family with you." Pinecrest, a local county home for those who cannot live on their own, was not far from my home, but I knew little about them. So I went there and asked them if we could visit with our family. They were encouraged by my offer because these people did not get many visits. We visited every week for seven years. Every so often we had several of them over for dinner in our home. We had become their friends, and each one of our children had special people they visited each week.

I remember one special old woman, Muriel. Our son Zach was only six years old and he played checkers with Muriel each week, and she would let him win. One day Muriel was taken to the hospital and put into the intensive care unit (ICU). Normally only family are allowed to visit someone in ICU, but Muriel did not have any family. She was dying, and she would die alone. The nurses knew this, and they just let us all go in to visit. As she laid there in her bed, barely able to talk, she whispered to Zack with tears in her eyes, "I love you." A few days later she died.

We all long to have our lives filled with loving family members. We all want the comfort of coming home to a house of our loved ones. There is no substitute for family. But sitting home alone, overwhelmed with loneliness, does not improve by staying cooped up. Pursuing the needs of others is good medicine for a lonely heart. Loneliness exists because we live in a fallen world that is starving for the love of others. So we should all be reaching out to others in love. We can do this whether we are lonely ourselves or not.

We were created by God with a basic need to be loved, and a basic need to love others. We cannot make anyone love us, but we can chose to fulfill the second need, to love others. We just have to do it. Pray and ask God to show you where to go and who to love and how to love them.

God wants us to reach out in love for others. Most of us have the ability to reach out to others to fulfill our need to love. And when we love others, we usually find that our need to be loved is also fulfilled. When we are depressed, the best medicine is to focus on how we can be a blessing to someone else. Paul spoke about reaching out to the weak and concluded with Jesus' words that being a blessing is a blessing to ourselves.

In all things I have shown you that by working hard in this way we must **help the weak** and remember the words of the Lord Jesus, how he himself said, **'It is more blessed to give than to receive.'"** Acts 20:35 (ESV)

Teens are in a constant struggle to be accepted. Several years ago we were in a church that did not have any youth leaders, so my wife and I teamed up with another couple to head one up. We decided that this was not going to be a group that attracted youth with dynamic outings. We wanted the foundation for our time together to be based on a relationship with God and true relationships with one another.

There were several struggling teens at the time. Two were experiencing the rejection and divorce of their parents. Two others struggled with alcohol and drugs. Three others struggled with having their father legally removed from the home because he was accused of sexual abuse. The pains were immense, and for each one of them, they had to suffer alone without the support of their family because their family was the source of their struggles.

These were young people ranging from about fourteen to twenty-two. Our weekly meetings had some simple principles.

- We would provide biblical teachings that were based on real life situations. Jesus came for real life.
- Our meetings, including teaching, would be highly interactive. We met together to have relationships. We would teach with open-ended questions and encourage discussion with varying personal perspectives and experiences.
- Teaching was not to be academic, like school. It was to be applicable to the lives of those present. This meant that everyone was encouraged to share their life with others.
- We would use part of our time to break down into small groups of three to six so that everyone would have a chance to relate what was going on in their lives and to be heard.
- Once a month we would do something fun together, such as canoe, a scavenger hunt, or anything that they chose. We would also have service projects to serve others in the church congregation, such as raking leaves for the elderly, or any home projects that required several energetic youths.

This youth group became much more than a weekly meeting. These young people became close friends that came alongside of each other in their struggles. They were there for each other at school. They planned other activities together throughout the week. The youth group was only for two years, but they maintained active relationships for years later. Today they are all young adults going in different directions, but they are still connected.

The evidence of what this group was doing in each other's lives became very apparent when we met for "circle time". At youth group, once every month or so, we formed one large circle of chairs so that we faced each other. We had a card with a question on it and passed it around the circle as each one answered the questions. The questions were always about what God was doing in your life. As we sat in a circle of about twenty-five of us, and as the question came to each one, tears began to flow. Boys, with tears rolling down their cheeks, would express how they couldn't have made it through their family struggles without the loving support of one or two specific people in the group. Others would confess their struggles, knowing that they were in the presence of people who cared for them.

Many times we struggle through life thinking we are the only ones. We isolate our inner fears, pains and emotions because we do not think that others truly care or understand. But during "circle time" we experienced the freedom to come out of isolation and into a loving and accepting and understanding group of fellow human beings who cared about one another.

My wife and I along with the another couple who chose to lead this group did not volunteer because we were personally lonely or struggling. We each had one or two of our own children in this age group, so we became involved as responsible parents. We volunteered to lead as responsible servants. We did not go into this in order to get a blessing, but to bless others. But we became highly blessed. The four of us met weekly in addition to the weekly youth meeting to pray for the Lord's direction. Consequently, we became close spiritual friends. And we witnessed together how God was forming us as leaders and how God was transforming these youth and joining them together in love. My wife and I found that our home became a lively meeting place for many of these youth. They frequently just dropped in and socialized. Our home became a warm, inviting place to enjoy one another.

So what can we learn from this in our own personal battle with loneliness and depression? Serve and become a blessing to others. We were called to love and to be a blessing. (1 Peter 3:8-9) The measure that we use will be poured back out into our lives.

> Give, and it will be given to you: A good measure, pressed down, shaken together, running over, will be poured into your lap. For the measure you use will be the measure you receive. Luke 6:38 (NET)

Do you struggle with loneliness; then reach out to the lonely. Pray and ask God to show you where he wants you to serve others.

It has been said that we all have a love tank, and much of the time our tanks are running empty. There is no question that being loved by others has the potential to fill them up. But I have found that wounded people never seem to fill up, even when being loved by others. They continue to complain and focus on every shortcoming. *There is a mysterious solution to filling our own love tank—reach out to love others*. When we do this we are availing our lives to God so that he can love others through us. And when he pours out his love through us, our tank gets filled at the same time. It is like others get the overflow from our tank, so our tank gets filled up in the process.

God Has Become Our Comforter, Helper and Counselor

This discussion and these recommendations are not to take lightly the serious battles that we have against loneliness and depression that comes from them. The key is to recognize that it is a battle, and unless we fight against loneliness, it can overwhelm us.

Take heart! We are not alone in this battle against loneliness. Love is still available to us. God has chosen to give us his Holy Spirit to live within us. Our separation from God has been resolved. Our broken relationship has been reconciled. Jesus paid the price for a restored relationship with the living God. And from this power of the living, loving God living within us by his Spirit, we are empowered to love one another. This is the hope that we have in this life.

Just as we long for true and deep relationships with others, God longs for this same kind of relationship with us. In times of loneliness, seek God. He has not left us alone. He is more than just at our side; Jesus sent his Spirit to make his home within us. Seek him. Know him. Find peace in him. Rest in him. Find comfort in him. Talk with him. He knows you; know him.

> If you love me, you will keep my commandments. And I will ask the Father, and he will give you another **Helper**, to be with you forever, even the Spirit of truth, whom the world cannot receive, because it neither sees him nor knows him. You know him, for he dwells with you and will be in you.
> I will not leave you as orphans; I will come to you. Yet a little while and the world will see me no more, but you will see me. Because I live, you also will live. In that day you will know that I am in my Father, and you in me, and I in you. Whoever has my commandments and keeps them, he it is who loves me. And he who loves me will be loved by my Father, and I will love him and manifest myself to him. John 14:15-21 (ESV)

As this passage promises, Jesus has asked the Father to send us a Helper (ESV and NKJV). The Greek word is Paraclete, which is a difficult term to translate into English. The NIV, KJV and HCSB translated this Helper as our Counselor. The NET and NLT translated this Helper as our Advocate. And the ASV translated him as our Comforter. So we can conclude that Jesus did not leave us alone; he sent his Spirit to live with us and even in us to be our Helper, Counselor, Advocate and Comforter.

The Spirit wants to have a relationship with us, but we must also desire to have a relationship with him. This relationship is borne out in love—our love for one another. The Helper lives and loves through us. This is how we remain connected to Jesus and live in his love. This is the secret source of true and lasting joy.

If you obey my commands, you will remain in my love, just as I have obeyed my Father's commands and remain in his love. I have told you this so that my joy may be in you and that your joy may be complete. My command is this: Love each other as I have loved you. John 15:10-12 (NIV)

Loving others is the ultimate solution to most any depression of any cause.

Reflection Questions

How do you struggle with loneliness? What is your situation? Who do you miss?

How many good friends do you have? Describe your relationships with them. How often and how do you relate? Are you there for their loneliness?

How might you reach out to others to comfort them in their loneliness or struggles in this life? When and how will you start?

Is God lonely for you? Describe your intimacy with God. How are you intimate with Jesus by the Word of God, who is Jesus? (John 1:1) How are you intimate in prayer? How are you intimate with the body of Christ, where Jesus lives? (This is much more than going to church. This is one-on-one intimacy with a fellow Spirit-filled brother or sister in Christ.)

How are you loving others to meet their pain of loneliness?

Made in the USA
Columbia, SC
06 August 2024

40084261R00124